HAGGAI, ZECHARIAH, AND MALACHI

MESSAGES OF RENEWAL AND HOPE

Light to My Path Series

Old Testament

Ezra, Nehemiah, and Esther
Isaiah
Ezekiel
Amos, Obadiah, and Jonah
Micah, Nahum, Habakkuk, and Zephaniah
Haggai, Zechariah, and Malachi

New Testament

John
Acts
Romans
Philippians and Colossians
James and 1 & 2 Peter
The Epistles of John and Jude

Haggai, Zechariah, and Malachi

Messages of
Renewal and Hope

F. Wayne Mac Leod

Authentic
MEDIA

Authentic Media
We welcome your comments and questions.
129 Mobilization Drive, Waynesboro, GA 30830 USA authenticusa@stl.org
and 9 Holdom Avenue, Bletchley, Milton Keynes, Bucks, MK1 1QR, UK
www.authenticbooks.com

If you would like a copy of our current catalog, contact us at:
1-8MORE-BOOKS
ordersusa@stl.org

Haggai, Zechariah, and Malachi
ISBN: 1-932805-16-8

09 08 07 06 05   6 5 4 3 2 1

Published in 2005 by Authentic Media

Cover design: Paul Lewis
Interior design: Angela Duerksen
Editorial team: Bette Smyth, Karen James, and Carol Johnson

Printed in United States of America

Contents

Malachi

Preface

What an awesome privilege the Lord has given
me to write these devotional commentaries. I
have often found myself praising the Lord for
the things I have been learning from him as I write. It is my
prayer that God will bless you as you read this book as much
as he has blessed me in writing it.

The prophecies of Haggai, Zechariah, and Malachi are
as relevant to us today as they ever were. Haggai spoke to
a people who were caught up in building their own homes
while neglecting the work of God. They were missing
the blessing of God because they did not put him first in
their lives. The rebuilding of the temple invited the return
of God's presence to his people and looked forward to a
glorious future of peace and prosperity.

Zechariah challenged his people to live in the reality of
the coming judgment of God on unbelief. He reminded them
of the wonderful blessings that could be theirs if only they
would reach out and accept what their God wanted to offer
them. He told them of the incredible love of God for his

people and reminded them that the day was coming when the great Messiah would come to bring them a rich and full salvation.

Malachi addressed a people who had lost the joy of worship and service. Instead, they had yielded to the temptations of the world, driving away the blessing of God. To these rebellious people, the prophet promised that the Messiah would come to refine and purify. The prophet called his people to repentance and renewal in light of God's purposes for them.

I trust that the words of these prophets will speak very personally to you as you read this book. I would encourage you to take the time to read the Bible passage listed at the beginning of every chapter. This commentary is not the Bible. My interpretations are not the only way of seeing the truths of these prophecies. My intention is not to be intellectual but rather to focus on how these books apply to our lives today.

May God richly bless you as you seek him in this commentary.

F. Wayne Mac Leod

Haggai

1

Consider Your Ways

Read Haggai 1:1–15

This is the prophecy of Haggai. There are only two references to this man in the rest of Scripture. Both of these references are found in the Book of Ezra (Ezra 5:1; 6:14). Haggai lived at the time when the people of God were returning home from their long captivity in Babylon. Led by Zerubbabel, Ezra, and Nehemiah, they returned to their homeland to rebuild the ruins of Jerusalem and the temple. Haggai spoke into this context. You can imagine the mixture of feelings as the people began the long process of rebuilding their once-glorious city. God's people were happy to be home, but there was much work to be done to restore the city after it had been destroyed by the enemy.

Verse 1 tells us the exact date of the prophecy of Haggai. It was on the first day of the sixth month of the second year of the reign of Darius the king of Persia. (At this time Israel was part of the Persian Empire.) It was on this exact day that the word of the Lord came to Haggai the prophet. God had something to say to his people and in particular to the leaders of his people at that time. This prophecy was intended for Zerubbabel the governor and Joshua the high priest.

Verse 2 shows us something of the attitude of the people of Jerusalem in Haggai's time. They had been saying that it was not yet time to rebuild the house of the Lord. There were many things that needed to be done to restore the city of Jerusalem. The house of the Lord would have to wait. Notice here that the people of God had not completely ruled out the rebuilding of the house of the Lord. The problem was really a matter of priority. They felt that there were more important things to do first. Verse 4 shows us some of their priorities.

Notice in verse 4 that the people, or at least the governor and high priest, were living in their nicely paneled homes, but they did not have time to rebuild the house of God. When everything else was taken care of, they would find the time for the Lord and his house.

Could it be that there are many people in our day living like the people of Haggai's day? Many times I have shared the gospel with individuals who said, "It's not time for me to accept the Lord. Give me a few more years to enjoy myself before I make a commitment to him." Are there things that you need to do for the Lord that you have been putting off? Maybe you got up this morning and said, "I just don't have time for the Lord right now; but when I get home, I'll see if I can find a moment to spend with him." Maybe it's the way you are using your finances. Could it be that you are spending your resources on yourself and ignoring the great need of finances for the expansion of the gospel? There are many ways we can be guilty of the same sin as the people of God in the days of Haggai. It's not that we aren't concerned about the Lord and his work. It's just that other things have taken priority.

Having stated the problem, God challenged the people to consider their ways: "Give careful thought to your ways," (verse 5). God told them to take a moment to consider their priorities. To help them in their thoughts, God gave them some particular things to think about in verse 6, "You have planted much, but have harvested little. You eat, but never have enough. You drink, but never have your fill. You put on clothes, but are not warm. You earn wages, only to put them in a purse with holes in it."

If they had considered these matters, they would have had to admit that there was a general lack of blessing in their lives. They didn't seem to be getting anywhere. They worked hard but had nothing to show for it. Things just didn't seem to be going their way. It's not that things were terrible—they were certainly happy to be in their own land—but they were not experiencing the wonderful blessing of God. Something needed to change. The challenge of the Lord came in verse 8, "Go up into the mountains and bring down timber and build the house, so that I may take pleasure in it and be honored."

For these individuals the mountain was a literal mountain, and the wood was literal wood. They needed to get to work and cut the wood necessary to build the temple. What are the mountain and the wood for you today? Notice in verses 9–11 that as long as the people did not place God first in their lives, they lacked blessing. They expected much, but they saw so little. What they brought home God blew away. They never seemed to prosper. This happened because they did not care about the house of God, and, more importantly, they did not place God as the highest priority in their lives. Because they did not take care of the house of God, the Lord withheld from them the dew of heaven. The crops failed in the ground. God called for a drought on the fields, mountains, and the grain. This drought also touched their new wine and oil as well as their crops. Everything was affected by this drought. People, livestock, and all the labors of their hands suffered because the work on the house of God was neglected.

This same principle is true today. Neglect your spiritual life and your family life will suffer. Neglect the Lord and the impact of that will be seen in your work and business. Ignore your relationship with God and you will suffer in every other area of your life as well. Our spiritual life affects everything we do. The challenge here is to see the importance of our spiritual development. We cannot afford to ignore our relationship with the Lord. When things get more and more hectic at work, we need more and more time with the Lord outside of work. When trials and temptations come rushing in on us, we especially need to take time with the Lord. Often, however, the Lord is neglected.

Haggai challenged the people of God to get their priorities straight. Notice in verse 12 that Zerubbabel, Joshua, and all the returned exiles heard what the Lord said to them through Haggai. They heard the message because the Lord had sent Haggai and because the people feared the Lord. It is true that these people had been neglecting their spiritual responsibilities; however, they did love the Lord. They were still open to hearing what the Lord had to say. When God sent his servant, they recognized that he was truly from God, and they took what he said seriously.

Verse 14 tells us that when Haggai spoke the word, the power of the Lord stirred up the people to hear and obey. Ultimately, it was not the eloquent words of Haggai but the power of God that won the hearts of his people. Just three weeks later, the rebuilding of the temple began. Haggai was the instrument that God used to stir the people to do the work. The fruit was ripe for the picking. Haggai was obedient to the voice of the Lord. God used the spoken word of his servant Haggai to rouse his people to action.

This chapter calls us to consider our own priorities. Are our priorities right? May God challenge us to live and walk with the right priorities.

For Consideration:

- What does this passage teach us about priorities in our lives as believers?

- What do we learn here about the power of the spoken word?

- Are there any areas in your life where you need to reorganize your priorities to put God first?

- What is the result of not putting God first in our lives?

For Prayer:

- Ask God to help you see those areas in your life where you have not put him first.

- Thank him that he is very patient with us, even when we are too busy to spend time with him.

- Ask God to heal your nation and bring it back to the Lord and his priorities.

2

The Glory of This House

Read Haggai 2:1–9

We saw in the last meditation that the people of God were ready to go to the mountains and bring down the timber necessary to repair the temple. As the reconstruction took place, there was a mixed reaction. Some of the older people remembered the temple of Solomon and all its splendor. They were not at all impressed with this new temple. In comparison, this temple seemed inferior. Deep down they were grieved in their hearts at the sight of this "lesser" temple.

It is in this context that the word of the Lord came to Haggai on the twenty-first day of the seventh month. This was less than a month after the construction began (see Haggai 1:15). God told Haggai to speak to Zerubbabel the governor, Joshua the high priest, and the remnant of the people. He was to ask them a series of questions. The nature of the questions shows us what was happening in the minds of those who were building the temple: Who saw the temple in its former glory? How does this temple appear to you compared to the former temple? Does this temple seem to be like nothing to you?

There was a general discouragement among the people. Obviously, the enemy was not happy to see the work of the Lord moving ahead, and so he sowed seeds of dissatisfaction among the people. You can imagine how this would have affected the work of the temple. As the older people began to comment on the smallness of this work, those working on the temple would have been disheartened.

Something else needs to be mentioned here. The enemy was attacking the work by causing the people to look to the glory of the past. The older people were particularly prone to this temptation. They wanted things to be like they were in the past. The work of God must go forward. Doing things the way they have always been done is not necessarily the solution. How often has the enemy trapped us in our traditions? All our effort can be spent on trying to keep things the way they have always been. We frown on anything new. We resist the new work that God is doing. We cannot accept the new expressions of faith. We discourage creativity when it comes to new music and worship styles. The individuals who had seen the former glory of Solomon's temple were unwilling to change. What was good enough for Solomon was good for them. In reality, they were discouraging the younger generation. They were hindering the work of God.

God was not interested in repeating what happened in the days of Solomon. God wanted to do a new thing in their midst. Yes, the temple building was not like it was in the days of Solomon, but "I am with you," said the Lord (verse 4). Isn't that all that really matters? The structure would be different, but God would still be there.

Haggai reminded the people in verse 5 that God had made a promise to them when they left Egypt that he would not leave them. While the setting was going to be different,

God's Spirit would remain with them. They were not to be afraid or discouraged. They were to continue working on the temple as God was leading them.

Moving into something new is never easy. We have to turn to God, be strong, and obey in our current circumstances, rather than rely on our past experiences and history. Our confidence must be in the presence of God with us.

In verse 6 God made a wonderful promise to his people: In a little while, he would come and shake the heavens and the earth, as in the days of Moses when the Lord descended on Mount Sinai (Exodus 19:16–18). Whole nations would be shaken. The "desired of all nations" would come and fill the temple. Who is the desire of nations? It is none other than the Lord himself. The very presence of God would come and fill the temple. Admittedly, the temple was not as glorious in physical appearance, but it would be glorious in that the presence of God would be even more present than it was in the temple of Solomon.

This temple would not have as much silver and gold as did the temple of Solomon, but gold and silver did not make a temple glorious. God owned all the silver and gold anyway (see verse 8). How can we give him something that he already owns? In reality, the Lord was saying, "I don't need your silver and gold. I own it all anyway." The glory of this temple would not be seen in its physical appearance, but rather in the presence of the Lord descended on it. This temple would be even more glorious than the former temple because God would dwell in it.

God does not need fancy buildings. How often have we seen wonderful structures emptied of the presence of God? They are richly decorated, but they are not glorious in the biblical sense. It is the presence of God that makes a church beautiful and glorious. This new temple would be glorious in that sense.

God was going to do a wonderful work. It was a new

work, totally different from the work he did in the days of Solomon. In this new temple, the Lord would grant peace (verse 9). What a wonderful encouragement this would be to a people returning from a long captivity. They wanted no more war. They had seen the results of war. God was promising them peace. This peace would come through the desire of nations, who would dwell with them and fill their temple.

This wonderful new work would be a work done in simplicity. It would not have all the trappings of wealth and prosperity. It would be blessed by God, however, and as such would be very powerful.

For some believers, the events of verses 6–9 cannot be accounted for in history and so speak of a future time when God will shake the whole world, and Christ will come back to earth to rule over a glorious kingdom of peace from Jerusalem.

For Consideration:

• How does the enemy seek to discourage the work of the Lord in this passage? Have you seen evidence of this in your life or church?

• Why is it so hard to let God do a new work in our lives?

• Is there evidence of the presence of God in your church? What is that evidence?

• What makes a church glorious according to this passage?

For Prayer:

• Have you ever been guilty of discouraging the work that God wants to do because it was not as you expected? Ask God to forgive you and give you the ability to accept what he wants to do.

- Ask God to fill you with his Holy Spirit. Ask him to fill your church with the power and the presence of the Holy Spirit.

- Pray that the Lord would again shake the heavens and the earth and descend. Ask him to do a new work in your life.

- Ask the Lord to forgive you for the times you failed to see the wonderful work he was doing in your midst, as did the people of Haggai's day.

3

Unmerited Favor

Read Haggai 2:10–23

The word of God again came to the prophet Haggai on the twenty-fourth day of the ninth month. God spoke a number of times to his servant Haggai. This book is a series of messages given by God to the prophet over a period of about three months.

Notice that the message came to the prophet by means of a question (verse 11). The question was recorded in verse 12. God asked his people to imagine an individual carrying consecrated meat in the fold of his garment. As he carried the meat, it touched some bread, stew, wine, oil, or some other food. The question was this: if this consecrated meat touched something common, would the touched object become holy?

To understand what is being asked here, it is helpful to refer to the law of Moses recorded in Leviticus 7:19–21, "Meat that touches anything ceremonially unclean must not be eaten; it must be burned up. As for other meat, anyone ceremonially clean may eat it. But if anyone who is unclean eats any meat of the fellowship offering belonging to the LORD, that person must be cut off from his people. If anyone touches something unclean—whether human uncleanness or an unclean animal or any unclean, detestable thing—and then eats any of the meat of the fellowship offering belonging to the LORD, that person must be cut off from his people."

Let's return to the question asked in verse 12. Consecrated meat would not consecrate the object it touched. In fact, the consecrated meat would become unclean by touching something common. The law clearly stated that if consecrated meat touched something that was defiled or common, it was not to be eaten. The meat itself was to be burned. Anyone who ate that meat was to be cut off from the people of God.

The Lord asked a second question: if a person who was unclean (by coming into contact with a dead body) touched an object, would that object become defiled? The law clearly stated that something unclean would make any object it touched unclean.

Having asked these questions, the Lord told his people that this same principle applied to his people. As a people, they had become unclean through their disobedience of not rebuilding the temple. Everything they touched and everything they did was unclean because they themselves were unclean. Their sacrifices and offerings, like the consecrated meat, were clean in themselves but became unclean in the moment of contact with the unclean person. Everything these unclean people touched became unclean.

There is something very important for us to understand here. If we are not right with God, then everything we offer to him is unclean. The New Testament is very clear on this point. If I am not right with my brother or sister in Christ, God will not accept my offering (Matthew 5:23–24). If I do not treat my wife with respect, my prayers will not be answered (1 Peter 3:7). My service for God can become unclean because of my attitudes and sinful ways. If I want my offerings and service for God to be pleasing in his sight, I must be clean myself. How important it is that I strive to be pure and right before God in all things. In Haggai's day God's people were unclean, and, because of this, God could not accept their service and worship (verse 14).

The Lord called his people to consider what things had been like when they had turned their backs on God and refused to rebuild the temple. God reminded them of how he had struck their land and gardens with blight, mildew, and hail. Everything they touched as a people was defiled. The blessing of God was removed from the land. When they had expected twenty measures of grain, they only found ten. When they had gone to a wine vat to draw out fifty measures, they could only find twenty. Their disobedience had stripped them of the blessing of God in all areas of their lives.

The obedience of the people to rebuild the temple would cause God's blessings to be released. From the day that the foundation of the temple was laid, the blessing of God would again come to his people. Blessings would come because the Israelites were in a right relationship with God again. We can compare this to a branch fallen into a river. That branch hinders the natural flow of the river. So it was with God's people. There was a branch in their lives that was hindering the blessing of God from flowing. The moment they removed that branch, the blessing of God was showered down on them. What hinders the blessing of God in your life today?

In verse 20 the word of God again came to Haggai. He was to speak specifically to Zerubbabel the governor. God was going to shake the heavens and the earth. He was going to overturn royal thrones and shatter the power of foreign kingdoms. He would overthrow chariots and their drivers. Horses and riders would fall by the sword. God was about to do something very powerful. Zerubbabel was going to be the center of that activity. He was going to be God's chosen servant. He would be God's signet ring.

A signet ring was worn by a king and used to give his authority to a document. A king would seal a declaration by stamping his ring into the clay or wax tablet on which it was written. Sometimes a king would give his ring to a trusted servant who could then act on the king's behalf. Zerubbabel was being given authority to act on God's behalf. God would use him as his instrument to do a wonderful work in his day.

The prophecy of verses 21–23 was not fulfilled in the days of Zerubbabel. As a descendent of David, Zerubbabel represented the Davidic line of kings in post-exilic Israel. To encourage this disheartened community, the Lord gave them a promise of hope, renewal, and future glory that he would literally fulfill in his own time through a descendant of Zerubbabel, the Lord Jesus.

As we read this passage, we cannot help but be struck with the way God wants to bless his people. The moment the hindrances are removed, blessings are poured out in abundance. God was willing to shake the nations for his people. He was going to overthrow the powers of the nations before them.

We serve the same God today. I believe that there are blessings he delights to pour down on us in our day. He is willing to shake the heavens and the earth for us. Like the children in the days of Haggai, however, we need to be in a right relationship with him. The moment we turn to him, his blessings will fall on us.

For Consideration:

• What does this passage teach us about the importance of being right with God?

- What stands between you and the blessing of God today?

- What do we learn here about God's desire to bless his people?

For Prayer:

- Ask God to show you what stands between you and his blessings.

- Thank him that he is a God who delights in blessing his people.

- Ask him to pour out that blessing into your life and ministry.

Zechariah

4

The Four Horns

Read Zechariah 1:1–21

This is the prophecy of Zechariah. Verse 1 tells us that the word of the Lord came to him on the eighth month of the second year of King Darius of Persia. This places Zechariah at the time of Haggai, who also prophesied in the second year of Darius. At this time the people of God were returning to the land of Israel after seventy years of exile. Zechariah called the restored community to repentance while reassuring them of the hope of future blessings.

The Lord began by telling Zechariah that he was angry with his ancestors. From verse 4 we understand the reason for this anger. God had sent his prophets to the Israelites to warn them of their evil ways, but they had refused to listen. God was renewing his call to Zechariah's generation: "Return to me, . . . and I will return to you" (verse 3).

Notice here that the people were to return to God before he would return to them. There is a condition attached to the Lord's returning to them. Their sin and their rebellion had formed a barrier between them and God. God wanted to pour out his blessing on them, but their sin stood in the way. There is a great obligation placed on each and every one of us. To a large extent I can, by my rebellion or my surrender to the Lord, determine the condition of my spiritual life. As I surrender to him, he comes and fills my life. The Bible tells us not to grieve the Holy Spirit (Ephesians 4:30). There are many ways that I can resist the Holy Spirit of God in my life. This is what the people of God were doing in the days of Zechariah. God called them to return to him and surrender their lives and hearts to him. When they did so, the Lord would fill them and bless them again.

We are the biggest hindrances to the blessing of God in our lives. If only we would surrender to him, he would fill our lives with his richest blessings. If my society would but return to God, it too would experience his returning to them. If my church would repent of their evil ways and get right with God again, he would surely return, and we would again know the blessing of his presence in our midst.

Zechariah warned his people not to be like their ancestors who refused to return to the Lord. "Where are these individuals now?" asked the Lord. They were no longer alive. Even the prophets who spoke to them had passed on. They were judged for their evil deeds and sent into exile in Babylon. When they were judged, they repented of their evil, but it was too late to avoid judgment. Judgment had already come. God gave them what they deserved, according to his words and decrees which he commanded (verse 6). The people of Zechariah's day understood this judgment. They were just returning from seventy years of exile and finding their temple and city in ruins. They knew that this exile had been the judgment of God against their disobedient ancestors.

God's people were asked to remember what had happened to their ancestors, lest they too fall into the same trap. God's people had a choice to make. They could return to the Lord and his ways and see the Lord return to them, or they could follow the example of those who went before them and fall under the judgment of God.

Having thus challenged his people, Zechariah told them about a vision he had on the twenty-fourth day of the eleventh month of the second year of King Darius. In this vision that came at night, Zechariah saw a man riding a red horse. The color red in the Scriptures can symbolize judgment (Isaiah 63:2–3; Revelation 6:4). The horse and its rider were standing among myrtle trees in a ravine. It is unclear if there is any significance to the myrtle tree in this passage. Behind this man on the horse were other horses. They were red, white, and brown in color (verse 9). Zechariah did not understand the significance of these horses and what they were doing. He asked the angel who was talking with him about the meaning of this vision.

The angel explained to Zechariah that these riders were the ones the Lord had sent throughout the whole earth (verse 10). From the context we understand that they were sent to see what was happening on the earth and to report to the angel of the Lord (see verse 11). When they returned from their mission, they approached the angel of the Lord who was also standing among the myrtle trees. They reported that they had accomplished their mission and that they had found the earth at peace and rest.

Hearing their report, the angel of the Lord asked: "Lord Almighty, how long will you withhold mercy from Jerusalem and from the towns of Judah, which you have been angry with these seventy years?" (verse 12). The angel of the Lord was grieved to see the plight of the people of God, especially when he realized that the nations that sent them into captivity were living in peace and rest. Have you ever wondered why it is that the unbeliever seems to live in more prosperity than the believer? Have you ever wondered why some unbelievers seem to have fewer struggles in life than those who love the Lord? This was the struggle in the heart of the angel of the Lord. Why were the unbelievers at peace when God's people struggled so deeply?

As Zechariah listened in his vision, he heard the Lord comfort the angel who grieved for his people. Then the angel told Zechariah to speak to the people and tell them that the Lord Almighty was very jealous for Jerusalem and very angry with the nations who felt secure in their rebellion (verses 14–15). Notice here that while these nations were presently at ease, their security would not last. The angel told Zechariah that these world powers had mistreated God's people with evil intent and added to the calamity of God's discipline of Israel in her exile.

There are many people like this in our day. They feel that because the Lord has not already judged them, they are safe. They continue to add one sin on another. They do not realize that as they do so, they multiply judgment on themselves.

The angel told Zechariah that God was going to return to Jerusalem with mercy. There in that city he would again rebuild his house. He would stretch out his measuring line over Jerusalem. The stretching out of the measuring line seems to refer to the reconstruction of the city of Jerusalem. The blessing of God would again be felt in the city and the nation as a whole. God was going to return to his people. The towns of Judah would again overflow with prosperity and blessing. The Lord would comfort his people who had suffered in exile. He would choose them to be his people again. He would be their God, and the world would know that God was among them.

What a comfort this must have been to the people of God returning to Jerusalem in ruins. For seventy years they had been separated from God and his blessings. They had, no doubt, asked many questions. They may have wondered where God was in all their sufferings. Maybe some had even lost any hope of ever seeing God work again in their midst. Maybe you too are feeling something similar. How long have you prayed for a loved one to come to know the Lord? How long have you prayed that the Lord would pour out his blessing on your church or your nation? We all have issues for which we have sought the Lord long and hard. This passage gives us hope. The Lord promised to return to his people. He was watching over them and was jealous for them. He would not abandon them in their struggle.

In his vision, Zechariah looked up and saw four horns. Again he was confused as to the significance of these images. He asked the angel what they represented. The angel told him that these horns represented the four nations that had scattered Judah, Israel, and Jerusalem (verse 14). While we are not absolutely sure as to the identity of these particular nations, they may refer to the nations of Egypt, Assyria, Babylon, and Persia.

As Zechariah continued in his vision, he saw four craftsmen. He asked the angel what these craftsmen were coming to do. The angel told him that these craftsmen had come to terrify the horns and to throw them down (verse 21). We are not given the identity of these craftsmen who would throw down these nations. God was telling his people that the nations who had oppressed them would be destroyed.

What is important for us to see in this passage is that the Lord had not forsaken his people, even though they had turned their backs on God and had suffered the consequence of their sin (exile). They had received the punishment they deserved. Although the exile was over and many Israelites had returned home, they were still dominated by a foreign power (Persia). But if Israel returned to the Lord, he would restore his blessings on their devastated homeland. God does not forget his people. His blessings await those who will simply return to him.

For Consideration:

- Do you have unanswered prayers? What comfort do you take from this passage?

- Are there ways in which we too need to return to the Lord as his people? What are they?

- Why do you suppose the Lord waited so long before restoring the blessing to his people?

- What particular blessing are you seeking from the Lord?

For Prayer:

- Thank the Lord that although he does discipline his people, he will not forget them.

- Thank him that he does forgive us for our sins and shortcomings and restore us to fellowship with him.

- Ask him to restore his blessing to your life, your church, and your nation.

- Ask him to cause his people to return again to him to seek his face.

5

Roused from His Holy Dwelling

Read Zechariah 2:1–13

In chapter 2, Zechariah described yet another vision he saw. In this vision he saw a man with a measuring line in his hand. He asked the man where he was going with this line and was told that he was going to measure the city of Jerusalem to see how long and how wide it was. We are not clearly told why the measurements of the city were being taken, but we have already seen this measuring line in Zechariah 1:16, "Therefore, this is what the LORD says: 'I will return to Jerusalem with mercy, and there my house will be rebuilt. And the measuring line will be stretched out over Jerusalem,' declares the LORD Almighty." In chapter 1 we saw that the Lord promised that the city of Jerusalem would be rebuilt. The measuring of the city very likely had something to do with this restoration since a measuring line is a construction tool.

As Zechariah watched in his vision, the angel he was speaking with left him to speak with a second angel.

Zechariah overheard this conversation that was going on between these two angels and recorded it. One angel was told to go and tell Zechariah that Jerusalem would be without walls because of the great number of livestock and people living in it. The fact that the city was without walls seems to be significant for at least two reasons. First, a city without walls was either a city that was open to the attacks of the enemy or simply had no enemy to attack it. In this particular case, the second option seems more likely. The Lord was going to deal with the enemies of his people who would then not need to set up protective walls. God himself would be their protection. Second, we see in this passage that the reason given for there not being any walls was that there were simply too many people and livestock for the city to contain.

Notice in verse 5 that the Lord promised to be a wall of fire around the city of Jerusalem. He would protect it from all harm. It is not without significance that at the time of this prophecy, the walls of the city were broken down. The man-made walls built to protect the city many years before had not been strong enough to keep the enemy out. This time, however, no enemy would be able to penetrate because God himself would be the protective wall around his people. Since Jerusalem has not been a city of safety for thousands of years and since God keeps all of his promises, we can expect that this promise has a future fulfillment.

What kind of walls do we put up to protect ourselves? We can build walls all around ourselves and our possessions but lose them all if God is not our wall of protection. When we are in God's will and he surrounds us as a flaming wall of fire, no enemy can penetrate. We are safe and secure. What a wonderful picture we have here.

As Zechariah listened to the conversation between the two angels, he heard a call go out to the scattered people of God. Because of their sin, they had been scattered to the four corners of the earth. They had been taken from the land God had given to their fathers and mothers. A call went out to them to return from the north (the place of their exile). They were called to return from the land of Babylon to the land God had promised them and their children (verses 6–7). The time of their exile was over. Maybe it is time for us to hear this call as well. We have been so long in our captivity that we no longer expect to be released. The call goes out to us now to return. Now is the time for us to be free.

Not only would the children of God be called back to their own land but also God would deal with those who had oppressed them (verses 8–9). As Zechariah listened to this conversation in his vision, he heard one of the angels say: "After he has honored me . . . I will surely raise my hand against them" (those nations that plundered Israel). There is some question among commentators as to the identity of the individual who is going to be honored here. Some see this as referring to the Messiah, who would be honored by his Father and become the judge of the nations that had plundered his people. The Father certainly honored the Lord Jesus, and his death on the cross did seal the judgment of the nations (Matthew 25:31–46).

What is important for us to see here is that the Lord was going to judge those who had harmed his people. He was going to raise his hand against them because anyone who touched his people touched the apple of his eye. God's people are precious in his sight. To harm the child is to hurt the father. Jesus put it this way in Matthew 25:40, "I tell you the truth, whatever you did for one of the least of these brothers of mine, you did for me."

How important it is for us to realize that whatever we do to the children of God, we are doing to God. God takes this matter very seriously in this passage. He was going to judge those who had hurt his people. God's people had been slaves to these nations, but God would reverse the roles. The nations that had plundered God's people would be plundered by God's people.

This was cause for great rejoicing in Zion. The Lord was going to restore the fortunes of his people. The Lord was going to come and make his presence known in their midst. Again they would be a glorious people. For this reason the children of God were to rejoice (verse 10). On the day when the Lord restored the blessing to his people, many nations would join them. God's people would no longer be only from one nation but from many nations (see verse 11). People from every tribe and nation would come to know this God of Israel and accept him as their God. We are some of those people. We too have come to know the God of Israel and have accepted him as our God.

God had not forgotten his people. He would once again inherit Judah (verse 12). He would take back the land that was his. He would again choose Jerusalem as his portion. The whole earth is called to be still before the Lord because he was about to rouse himself from his holy dwelling. He was going to act on behalf of his people. He was going to judge and restore the blessing taken from his people Israel by the enemy.

Many believers look to the future for the literal fulfillment of all these promises to Israel. They believe that Christ will return to earth, and, by simply raising his hand against the nations who have spoiled his people over the years, he will render these nations spoil to be plundered (see Revelation 19:15–18 for a similar image). Christ will return to Judah and Jerusalem, and Israel will know the Savior (see Isaiah 60:14–16 for a similar image).

As I examine this passage, I cannot help but ask myself, "What territory has the enemy taken from us today?" Are we too not like the children of Israel in the days of Zechariah? Because of our sin, we have lost much territory to the enemy. We are helpless before the enemy to reclaim that territory. Consider for a moment the sins that have infiltrated our churches and our society. This is territory lost to the enemy. Consider for a moment the number of believers held in bondage by some stronghold of sin in their life. This too is territory lost to the enemy. Consider the immorality in our society and the injustice that seems to be rampant all around us. Is this not territory lost to the enemy? The Lord promises to come to reclaim this territory. The time has come for us to escape the clutches of the "Daughter of Babylon." The time has come for the scattered sheep to return. God is coming to dwell in our midst. He is coming to restore his people to their former glory. He will again live among us. This is a day for rejoicing. This is a day for us to sing and be glad. The enemy will not prevail. God himself will be a fiery wall of protection around us. He will again restore the city.

For Consideration:

- What territory have we lost to the enemy?

- What blessings do we need to see restored to the people of God?

- What difference does the presence of God make in the life of a church or society? What causes God to withdraw his presence for a time?

For Prayer:

- Thank God for the promises here that he would restore the glory of his people.

- Thank him that he promises to be a wall of fire around his people.

- Ask him to forgive you for the times you have spoken harshly about one of the apples of his eye.

- Ask him to come to dwell among his people again.

6

Joshua
the High Priest

Read Zechariah 3:1–10

The vision of Zechariah continued. In his vision the prophet saw Joshua the high priest. Joshua stood before the angel of the Lord. We are not told why he was there, only that he had been summoned by the Lord to stand before him.

What Zechariah particularly noticed here in this picture was the presence of Satan standing beside Joshua and accusing him. We can only imagine what Joshua was feeling that day as he stood before the presence of a holy and awesome God with Satan standing beside him to accuse him. The purpose of Satan was to humiliate and deflate this chosen instrument of God. As Joshua stood before the Lord, he was humbled. He may have even felt deeply ashamed. Maybe some of the things that were being spoken were true. He knew that he was unworthy as a servant of God. Perhaps he felt the accusation of Satan very deeply. Maybe he wondered if he should even be standing in the presence of such a holy God. Maybe you have felt the sting of Satan's accusations yourself.

In his vision, Zechariah heard the Lord speak to Satan. "The LORD rebuke you, Satan! The LORD, who has chosen Jerusalem, rebuke you! Is not this man a burning stick snatched from the fire?" (verse 2). We are not specifically told what the response of Joshua was to this, but we can be assured that he was truly encouraged. The LORD himself, the God of his ancestors, had taken up his defense and rebuked the accuser.

Of particular significance was what God said about Joshua being a burning stick plucked from the fire (see verse 2). The fire seemed to represent the persecution that the people of God had been under as they were in exile. Joshua was one of these individuals who was plucked from the fire of God's judgment. He was one of God's chosen instruments taken from exile to rebuild the work of God in his "chosen Jerusalem." Satan was rebuked because he dared to speak out against God's favored people.

Of what use is a burnt stick? In reality it is useless. Yet this was the description of the individual that God was going to use. You may feel like you are a burnt stick. If God has chosen to use you, however, you are a chosen instrument.

Verse 3 tells us that as Joshua stood before the Lord that day, he was dressed in filthy clothes. He was in an embarrassing position. He had been through the fire of God's judgment, and as he stood before the Lord, he knew that he was not pure. Certainly in his condition he could not exercise his role as high priest. God demanded high standards of cleanliness and purity of all priests. Again, the angel of the Lord spoke to those standing nearby. "Take off his filthy clothes," he said. To Joshua he said: "See, I have taken away your sin, and I will put rich garments on you" (verse 4).

Joshua was filthy. He was far from perfect. He had

fallen short of the standard that God had set for him. God, however, was willing to forgive. He was willing to exchange those filthy clothes for new clean clothes of forgiveness and purity. What a wonderful truth we see here in this passage. None of us are worthy to stand before God and minister in his name. We stand humbled in his presence with our heads bowed. Satan stands by to accuse. What a blessing it is to know, however, that though we are unworthy, God has called us. In him we can be cleansed and clothed with everything we need. Satan's accusations fall short of their intended purpose to discourage and dishearten.

In his vision, Zechariah joined in, asking those around Joshua to put a clean turban on his head (verse 5). The word *turban* in the original language refers to the high priest's head covering. In calling for a turban to be placed on Joshua's head, Zechariah was asking for Israel's priestly place with God to be restored. An engraved gold plaque tied to the front of the turban read "HOLY TO THE LORD" (Exodus 28:36–37). God was renewing his call to Joshua as his holy high priest to his chosen nation, Israel.

As Satan stood beside Joshua with all his accusations, God rebuked him. In the presence of Satan, this servant of God was forgiven and clothed with the authority and holiness necessary to do the work that God had called him to do. Joshua had nothing to boast about in himself. He was unworthy, but God had chosen him and equipped him. What a wonderful privilege.

Joshua's calling could not be taken for granted. The angel of the Lord spoke to Joshua and told him: "If you will walk in my ways and keep my requirements, then you will govern my house" (verse 7). God was willing to forgive. He was willing to give Joshua the authority necessary for his calling. Joshua, however, was expected to obey the Lord and be faithful to him. His obedience to the Lord would allow him to remain in that authority. If he was faithful to his

Lord, then he would be given authority to govern the Lord's house. Joshua would be given charge of the temple courts and access to the presence of God, like the angels standing there with him.

How important it is for us to understand the connection here between obedience and authority. God grants his authority to those who will be faithful to him. In the parable of the talents, the master took his talents away from the one who did not make use of them and gave them to the one who had been faithful (Matthew 25:24–30). God is not interested in pouring out his authority on those who will not be faithful to him in the use of this authority. Obedience is vital. As those who have been chosen by God, we need to search our hearts to be sure that there is nothing that stands between our Lord's blessing and us.

In verse 8 the Lord addressed Joshua and his associates. The angel of the Lord told them that they represented greater things to come. God was going to send his servant "the Branch" who would come as a great high priest to minister to his people. That Branch was the Lord Jesus who is our Great High Priest anointed to bring us to God.

In Zechariah's vision a stone was placed in front of Joshua. That stone had seven eyes. Some translations read "seven faces." Seven is the number of fullness or perfection, possibly symbolizing complete, divine intelligence. There is some debate over the identity of this stone. This stone had an engraving on it indicating that the Lord would remove the sins of his people in a single day. The stone may have been a memorial stone with these words engraved on it, standing in the presence of the Lord as a reminder of his promise to bring forgiveness to Israel, "that land." The stone may also have represented the Messiah who was referred to as a stone (Ephesians 2:20; 1 Peter 2: 4–8).

Could it be that the stone that was placed before Joshua represented the Lord Jesus through whom the nation of

Israel would be offered forgiveness of their sin? Notice that this sin would be removed in a single day. The day the Lord Jesus died for our sins was the day that these sins would be removed. On that day forgiveness was offered for every sin. On a single day, his blood covered all our sins. On that day the backbone of the enemy was broken and the sinner set free. Since the nation of Israel rejected her Messiah at his first coming, this promise to "that land" of Israel awaits a future fulfillment. Messiah will return to earth and forgive Israel as a whole (Romans 11:26–27).

"In that day" the Lord promised that Israelites would invite their neighbors (Gentiles) to join them in celebrating the agricultural prosperity and peace of the Lord (see Isaiah 66:7–11 for a similar image). There are only two reasons for inviting your neighbor to sit under your vine and fig tree: to share in the blessing you have received from your vine and fig tree and to rejoice in the peace between you and your neighbor. Because of the work of Christ on the cross for sins, we too can experience this blessing and peace with those around us.

For Consideration:

- Have you ever been discouraged like Joshua in this passage? What encouragement do you find in this chapter?

- Have you experienced forgiveness of sin like Joshua? How can you know that you are forgiven?

- What is the connection between authority and obedience?

- What do we learn here about the kind of person the Lord can use?

For Prayer:

• Thank the Lord for the way he has chosen to bless and honor us as his children.

• Are there areas where you need to be obedient to the Lord? Ask the Lord to reveal to you any obstacles to blessing and authority in your life.

• Thank the Lord for the way he wants to forgive you and use you just as you are.

7

The Golden Lampstand

Read Zechariah 4:1–14

In chapter 4 the prophet Zechariah awoke from his sleep. He looked and saw a golden lampstand with a bowl on the top. Zechariah noticed that there were seven channels or pipes (NKJV) leading from the bowl to seven lamps possibly surrounding the bowl. The bowl obviously contained oil for the seven lamps. Zechariah also noticed that there were two olive trees, one on either side of the bowl. Quite possibly these trees supplied oil to the bowl. Zechariah was confused by what he saw. He asked the angel to explain the vision.

The angel gave Zechariah a message for Zerubbabel, who was a descendant of King David as well as the leader of the first group of returnees from exile and the governor of that first restoration community. God's word to Zerubbabel was that the work God had called him to do would be accomplished not by might or by power but by the Spirit of God (verse 6). In the power of the Spirit, Zerubbabel would do wonderful things. Oil in the Scripture often represents the ministry of the Holy Spirit. We see this connection in 1 Samuel 16:13. When David was anointed with oil, the Spirit of God came on him. We also see the term "anoint" used in connection with the ministry of the Holy Spirit in Isaiah 61:1 and Acts 10:38. Zerubbabel would be the vessel, but God's Spirit would be his strength.

"What are you, O mighty mountain?" asked the Lord (verse 7). The mighty mountains would be broken down and become level ground before Zerubbabel as he stepped out in the power of God's Spirit. There would be obstacles, but in the name of the Lord, Zerubbabel would overcome them. This message to Zerubbabel would have been encouraging as he led God's people in the difficult task of rebuilding both the temple and the community in Jerusalem. There was much opposition to this rebuilding (Ezra 4:1–5, 24).

Do you have any mountains in your life? Are there things that you just don't seem to be able to overcome? In our human strength, we cannot break down these mountains. They are simply too much for us. In the strength of his Spirit, however, great things can be accomplished. There is no mountain too big for his Spirit to overcome through us. When the Spirit of God is at work, what is humanly impossible becomes possible.

Zechariah was to tell Zerubbabel that not only would the mountains be broken down in the power of the Spirit of God but God would also enable Zerubbabel to bring forth the capstone with shouts of "God bless it" (verse 7). The capstone was the final stone to be placed in the building. When this stone was laid, the building was completed. God was telling Zerubbabel that not only would the obstacles be overcome for him in the power of the Spirit but also, by that same Spirit, the work on the temple that he had been called to do would be completed.

What a wonderful thing it is to know that the Lord who called us is also able to complete the work he has called us to do. What has the Lord called you to do? Trust in his Spirit. God will not leave you to face the obstacles alone. By his Holy Spirit, he will overcome for you the many mountains that stand in your way, and he will bring the work to completion. The capstone will be laid and God will be glorified. This is what the Lord told Zechariah in verse 9. Zerubbabel had laid the foundation of this temple, and his hands would complete it. All of this would be done by the power of God's Spirit working in him.

At this time the people of God were discouraged. Haggai 2 and Ezra 3 tell us that when the older generation saw the foundation of the temple being laid, they began to weep and grumble. This temple was not the same as the temple of Solomon. These individuals could not believe that the Lord's blessing would be on a temple that was so much smaller than the temple of Solomon. Zerubbabel would have heard these comments as he oversaw the construction of the temple.

In light of these things, Zechariah was told to speak to Zerubbabel and the people to tell them not to despise the day of small things (verse 10). This temple, though smaller, would be more glorious than the temple of Solomon (see Haggai 2). The Lord told them that the day was coming when men would rejoice to see the plumb line in the hands of Zerubbabel. The plumb line was used in construction. It would be hung from a height to assure that the walls were straight. The picture of Zerubbabel with the plumb line in his hands shows us that the work of the temple would begin again. Zerubbabel would use this plumb line to be assured that the work was being done as God required. He was given the responsibility to supervise this work.

Notice in verse 10 that the Lord God was also watching over the work of his temple. The angel reminded Zechariah that the eyes of the Lord were ranging throughout the entire earth. How often we feel that we are alone responsible to watch over the work that God has called us to do. God reminds us here that he too is watching over his work.

To some this temple was small and insignificant, but God was looking after it. God had a wonderful plan. This work may have seemed small and insignificant, but God was in it. God's people should not despise what God is watching over. God's blessing is on small things as well as big things. Maybe your ministry seems insignificant, but is God in it? If God is in it, it is a glorious ministry. God has often taken what appears to be small and insignificant and used it to accomplish great things for the sake of the kingdom. We should never despise small things when God is in them.

There is one final thing that Zechariah could not understand in his vision. He asked the angel to explain to him the significance of the two olive trees. The angel told him that these two trees represented the two anointed ones (literally, "sons of oil") who stood before the Lord. Who were these anointed ones? In the last two meditations, we read about the call of Joshua the high priest and the call of Zerubbabel the governor. These individuals were called of God to a particular ministry. In Israel only kings and priests were anointed with oil for their ministries. Many commentators see these anointed ones as Joshua and Zerubbabel. They were the two olive trees who would provide oil for the lamps. Could it be that the lamps were the people of God who were shining for him? Jesus told us that we are the light of the world (Matthew 5:14). We are called to shine into this world as bright witnesses for him. In order for the children of God to shine as witnesses for him, God has anointed his servants to feed and minister to each other. As people serve, their lights tend to grow dim. Joshua and Zerubbabel were anointed to minister to the other servants of God, keeping the fire alive in them. Are you one of those individuals whom God has called to be a channel of his oil? Realize the awesomeness of the task that he has given you.

There are many people who are depending on you. God has anointed you to be an olive tree supplying the oil of his blessing to his people.

Where does the strength come from to supply God's people with the oil they need to shine as lights? We have already seen what God told Zerubbabel in this chapter: it was not from his own resources that he would succeed. It was in the power of the Spirit of God that he could minister and complete his task. Only as we are rightly related to the Lord and draw on his infinite resources can we supply his people with the resources necessary to shine for him.

For Consideration:

- What is the difference between depending on our own strength and power and depending on the Lord? How can you tell the difference?

- What obstacles do you face in your ministry and Christian walk? What encouragement do you receive from God's word to Zerubbabel about the mountains becoming level ground?

- Are you a channel of blessing to the people of God? Explain.

- What does the Lord tell us here about small things? Is bigger always better? Explain.

For Prayer:

- Thank the Lord that he is in small things.

- Ask the Lord to help you to rely on his Spirit and not on your own strength to do the work he has called you to do.

- Has the Lord called you to be an "olive tree"? Ask him to fill you to overflowing so that you have all that is necessary to minister to his people.

8

The Scroll and the Basket

Read Zechariah 5:1–11

Zechariah's vision continued. This time he saw a flying scroll. This scroll was large in size. It was thirty feet long and fifteen feet wide (nine meters long and four and a half meters wide). This scroll would have been quite impressive to see because of its size. It was large enough for all to see.

As Zechariah looked at the scroll, the angel of the Lord told him that this scroll represented the curse of God that was going out over the land. On one side of the scroll was written: "Every thief will be banished," and on the other side was written: "Everyone who swears falsely will be banished" (verse 3). These curses reflect something of what was happening in the land at that time. There was disrespect for God and neighbors. The judgment of God was going to fall on Israel because of these sins.

This curse of God would be on the homes of those who were disregarding God's holy law. It would enter the home of the thief and of those who swore falsely in the name of the Lord. There this curse would remain until it destroyed the home with its timber and stones (verse 4). God took this matter very seriously. God's people would suffer the consequences of their sin.

It should be mentioned here that at this time the Lord was doing a new thing in their midst. The temple was being rebuilt. God was going to pour out his glory on the land. Before this could happen, however, sin needed to be cleansed from the land. God was purifying the land in preparation for his mighty work.

As he watched, Zechariah saw another object in his vision. This time he saw a measuring basket. The angel told him that this basket represented the sins of the people of Israel (verse 6). Zechariah noticed particularly that the basket had a lead cover. This was not typical. Obviously, it was important that the contents of this basket not escape to pollute the land.

Zechariah saw the angel lift the cover of the basket to reveal the contents. He saw a woman in the basket. "This is wickedness," said the angel (verse 8). When he said this, the angel pushed the woman back into the basket and closed the cover over her, so she would not escape.

The image here was that wickedness wanted to escape. The woman had to be forcibly pushed back into the basket. The cover was made of lead so that it could not be easily opened. Sin is always looking for a means of escape—it does not want to be restrained. You and I know how little it takes for anger and jealousy to come to the surface in our own hearts. How careful we need to be to keep it under control.

In verse 9 Zechariah looked up and saw two women approach with wind in their wings. The wind in their wings indicated that they were being carried along by the wind. Wind in Scripture often represents the Holy Spirit (John 3:8;

Acts 2:2–4). It could be that these women were being carried along by the Holy Spirit. They had a divine mission to accomplish and were being carried by the Spirit of God to accomplish a specific task. Zechariah described the wings of these women to be like the wings of a stork. Obviously, this is a reference to the large size of their wings. These women took the basket and flew away with it.

Zechariah asked the angel where the women were taking this basket. The angel told him that they were taking it to the country of Babylon, where they would build a house for it. There the basket would be kept. What we need to understand here is that Babylon was the place of exile for the people of God. Here they were oppressed and held in bondage. Revelation 17 and 18 describe for us a prostitute called Babylon who was going to be destroyed in the end times. Could it be that this woman is the same woman described for us in Revelation? What is important for us to note here is that this woman who represented wickedness would be taken away from the land of Israel. The land would be cleansed of wickedness. Notice that this woman was brought to the land of Babylon where she would dwell for a time. There she would be imprisoned. She was not destroyed, but she was held in bondage for a time. This was also part of God's cleansing of Israel in preparation for his work of renewal. According to Revelation 18, this Babylon would be finally destroyed. In the mean time, although she was bound, she still sought to lure the nations into her "adulteries" (Revelation 18:3).

It is encouraging to see that God is able to cleanse our land and our churches of this wickedness. The day is coming when God will deal finally with all the evil on the earth. What a wonderful day that will be. How we need to see him do this work in our own lives. Let us open our hearts for him to do this work.

For Consideration:

- What encouragement do you take from the fact that the Lord is able to bind evil and wickedness in our land?

- What in particular needs to be bound in your land or your church?

- What particular sin in your life needs to be put in that basket with the lead cover?

For Prayer:

- Ask the Lord to bind the evil in our land today.

- Thank him that he is Lord and that he will one day end all wickedness.

- Thank him that he is a holy and righteous God who hates evil.

9

Four Chariots
and a Crown

Read Zechariah 6:1–15

In this chapter the prophet Zechariah saw a vision of four chariots. These chariots came out from between two mountains of bronze. We are not given the identity of these two mountains. Verse 5 tells us that these chariots were coming from heaven. These mountains seemed to be a sort of gateway between heaven and earth.

In verses 2 and 3 we have a description of these chariots. Horses were pulling each of the four chariots. We are not told how many horses were pulling each chariot. The first chariot had red horses, the second had black horses, the third had white horses, and the fourth was drawn by dappled or gray horses. It is important to note that the apostle John also saw four horses of the same color in the book of Revelation. A quick look at Revelation 6 may give us a greater understanding of what these horses represented.

Concerning the red horse of Revelation 6:4 we read: "Then another horse came out, a fiery red one. Its rider was given power to take peace from the earth and to make men slay each other. To him was given a large sword." The red horse here symbolized war and bloodshed.

The black horse of Revelation 6:5–6 represented famine: "When the Lamb opened the third seal, I heard the third living creature say, 'Come!' I looked, and there before me was a black horse! Its rider was holding a pair of scales in his hand. Then I heard what sounded like a voice among the four living creatures, saying, 'A quart of wheat for a day's wages, and three quarts of barley for a day's wages, and do not damage the oil and the wine!'"

The white horse in Revelation 6:2 was a horse of conquest and vengeance: "I looked, and there before me was a white horse! Its rider held a bow, and he was given a crown, and he rode out as a conqueror bent on conquest."

The final horse was a dappled horse. John saw a pale horse (Revelation 6:8). The dappled horse was very likely of a grayish tone (pale in color). This horse represented death and plagues: "I looked, and there before me was a pale horse! Its rider was named Death, and Hades was following close behind him. They were given power over a fourth of the earth to kill by sword, famine and plague, and by the wild beasts of the earth."

It is quite likely that the horses and chariots Zechariah saw represented the various judgments of God that were going to fall on the earth. The angel told Zechariah that these horses were the four spirits of heaven who were going out from the presence of the Lord (verse 5). These horses and chariots were the servants of the Lord Almighty. They were beings sent out of heaven for a very particular purpose. They were his servants to exercise judgment on the earth.

The horses and chariots were given directions from the Lord. The black horses were to go to the north, the white horses to the west, and the dappled horses were to go to the south. Nothing is said here about the red horses and chariots and their direction.

Some see here a reference to Israel's enemies. Babylon lay to the north. Egypt was located to the south. To the west lay the coastland where the Philistines were located. God was going to deal with the enemies of his people. He was sending his chariots of wrath to defeat them.

As Zechariah watched the chariots, he could see that the horses were straining to go throughout the earth. They were eager to do the bidding of the Lord, but they were being restrained for a time. We see in verse 7 that it was only when the Lord told them to go that they were able to leave to accomplish their task.

For the moment the judgment of God was being restrained. The chariots of God's judgment were ready to be unleashed from the gates of heaven. All that was keeping them back was a word from the Lord. How long would God hold back his judgment? The day was coming when these horses would hear the word from the Lord and, bursting out of their stalls, they would rush forward to execute his judgment on the earth.

As the horses raced to their destinations, the Lord spoke to Zechariah. The horses going to the north gave God's Spirit rest in that land (verse 8). In what way was the Spirit of God given rest? Could it be that his Spirit had no rest until judgment was brought on the sin and evil of the land of the north? This may have represented judgment on Babylon.

After these events, the word of the Lord came again to Zechariah. He was told to take silver and gold from certain exiles who had returned from Babylon. He was to go to the house of Josiah the son of Zephaniah, where perhaps they were staying, and collect this offering. With it he was to make a crown and set it on the head of the high priest, Joshua. This command was somewhat unusual. The high priest wore a turban, never a crown. A crown was usually reserved for a king. The placement of a crown on the head of a priest would have been strange indeed. God was communicating something special through this action.

When he placed the crown on Joshua's head, Zechariah was to tell Joshua that God would raise up a man whose name was "the Branch" (verse 12). It is generally understood that this Branch was the Lord Jesus. Jesus would not only be a priest, but he would also be a king. Joshua would represent the Messiah who was to come as the Priest-King. Messiah would exercise the role of priest in that he would draw his people to the Father. He would also exercise the role of king in that he would set up a new kingdom and reign over it. Jesus would unite the priesthood with the role of king.

There are several things we learn about the Branch here. This individual would "branch out from his place" (verse 12). The place that is referred to here is Jerusalem. From Jerusalem his name would spread to the far corners of the earth. This Branch would "build the temple of the LORD" (verse 13). He would be clothed with majesty and rule on his throne as king. Not only would he sit on his throne as king but also as priest. The end of verse 13 tells us that there would be harmony between the two offices. There would no longer be a separate king and priest in Israel. Jesus would bring these two offices together as one. He would become a priestly king. The crown that Zechariah was to make was to be placed inside the restoration temple in Jerusalem as a reminder of the hope of the Messiah to come, who would become their priest and king.

Verse 15 tells us that those who were far away would contribute to the building of this temple. If the temple referred to here is the temple that was built in the days of Zerubbabel and Joshua, this prophecy would have been fulfilled as men such as Ezra and Nehemiah came from exile in Babylon to rebuild it. If the temple referred to here is the spiritual temple that the "Branch" would build, then we might see this as a reference to people from every nation that God is using to build the church today. Some believers hold that besides the spiritual temple and kingdom that Christ is building in the world today, there remains another physical temple and earthly kingdom presided over by Christ when he returns to Jerusalem at a future time.

We learn from this chapter that the Lord was going to send his horses of judgment to the nations that had oppressed his people. God, however, is not only a God of judgment but also a God of mercy and grace. He would also send a Messiah who would reign over his people as a priestly king. There was hope in him.

Notice that the chapter ends with the words: "This will happen if you diligently obey the LORD your God" (verse 15). This needs some explanation. The Lord had been challenging his people to rebuild the temple. He had been reminding them that the day was coming when the Messiah would come to reign in their midst and bring his peace. God's people would experience the fulfillment of these promises if they obeyed the Lord. God would help them to complete the temple, but they were going to have to set their minds to obey. God was going to send them the Messiah, but they would have to open their eyes and listen to him if they wanted to benefit from his reign. Certain of the blessings of God depend on our obedience. The Jews, for the most part, rejected the Messiah who came. In rejecting him they forfeited the blessing that was theirs in him at that time. Christ withdrew from national Israel until a future time when Israel will recognize him as Messiah (Matthew 23:37–39).

We too can forfeit by disobedience the blessing God wants to give us. There are blessings that God wants us to have, but to receive them we must learn to live in obedience. God's people in Zechariah's day were challenged to live in obedience and experience the richness of the blessing of God. Otherwise they would miss out.

For Consideration:

- What holds back the judgment of God today?

- Have you trusted the Messiah? How can you know that you have trusted in him and that you will be spared the judgment of the chariots of God?

- How can it be said that Jesus is both priest and king?

- What is the connection here between obedience and blessing?

For Prayer:

- Thank the Lord that he is sovereign over sin and evil and that he will one day judge this world.

- Do you know people who have never accepted Jesus as their priest and king? Ask the Lord to reveal himself to them.

- Ask the Lord to reveal to you any way in which you have missed his blessing by disobedience.

10

The True Fast

Read Zechariah 7:1–14

I t was in the fourth year of King Darius on the fourth day of the ninth month that this particular word of the Lord came to Zechariah. This was the month of Kislev, which commentators estimate to be around the first part of our month of December.

This word came to Zechariah when the people of Bethel sent individuals to seek the will of the Lord. They were wondering whether they should mourn and fast in the fifth month, as they had done for many years. The fast of the fifth month was in remembrance of the day the first temple was destroyed. The people of God had remembered this day throughout their seventy years of exile. Now that their exile was over and the new temple was being rebuilt, they were wondering if they should celebrate this fast anymore.

To find an answer to this question, they sent their representatives to the priests and the prophets (see verse 3). God would often speak to these individuals and communicate his will for the people. The very fact that the people were actually seeking the will of the Lord in this matter was a positive sign. They were concerned about what God wanted for them and their nation.

It was in this context that the word of the Lord came to Zechariah. God told him to ask the people of the land and the priests a question regarding the fast they had kept for those seventy years in exile. The Lord's question was this: "When you fasted and mourned in the fifth and seventh months for the past seventy years, was it really for me that you fasted?" (verse 5).

We have seen that the fast of the fifth month was a remembrance of the destruction of the temple by the conquering Babylonians. The fast of the seventh month mentioned in verse 5 was in remembrance of the murder of Gedaliah, the governor the Babylonians put in control over the people who were left in Israel during the exile (see Jeremiah 41:2).

It was true that during these months the people had fasted and mourned, but God was not impressed by these external signs of repentance. Instead, he saw deep into their hearts and knew that this fast had nothing to do with him. The people were not fasting and mourning because of their sin. They were fasting and mourning for themselves. They grieved because they were not in their land. They grieved because they were being held captive by the Babylonians. They were not grieving, however, because they had offended a holy God.

How easy it is for us to fall into the same trap. We may come to worship the Lord, but are we really worshiping him? Are we singing his praises because we love to sing or because we love our Savior? Are we preaching because we love to preach or because the Lord has burdened our heart with a word for his people? How much of what we do for the

Lord is really being done for ourselves? God is not fooled by outward appearance.

In answer to their question about whether they needed to continue to fast and mourn in the fifth and the seventh months, God responded by reminding them of the reason for the fast. He began by reminding them of the words of the prophets who spoke to their ancestors prior to the exile. At one time the land of Israel was at peace and prosperous. God's people, at that time, however, were not in a right relationship with him. God sent his prophets to warn them and to show them the way he intended them to live. Zechariah told those who stood before him that God had intended that they do the following four things (verses 9–10).

Administer justice. It was the will of God that his people administer justice in the nation. Justice demanded that individuals be treated with the dignity they deserved. Whether they were poor or rich, male or female, they were to be treated with respect and given their rights according to the law of God.

Show mercy and compassion. God wanted his people to have mercy and compassion, which extended beyond justice. While justice gave people what they deserved and what they had a right to receive, mercy extended its hand to those who did not deserve it. Mercy offered forgiveness and reached out in love to those who were unlovely.

Do not oppress. God told his people through Zechariah that they were not to oppress the widows, the fatherless, the foreigners, or the poor. God had these individuals on his heart. Obviously, these individuals were being cast aside. Their needs were not being met. They were being used to advance the cause of those who already had all they needed. The helpless and vulnerable in the society were being oppressed. God was angry with his people because of this.

Do not think evil in your hearts. Not only were the Israelites not to physically oppress other individuals, but they were not even to think evil about them in their hearts. Some might say, "As long as I don't physically oppress them, I can think what I want about them in my heart." Here God ruled out this possibility. There was no room for prejudice or bitterness in the heart of God's people toward one another.

These were the requirements that God had for his people. Verse 11 tells us that they refused to listen to the Lord and his prophets. They turned their backs on God and his word. Their hearts were as hard as flint stone. They would not listen to the words of the law of God that he spoke through his prophets. Because of this, the Lord was very angry and would not listen to them (verse 13). Then the Lord let Israel's enemies come and conquer.

This was the reason why the children of Israel had lost their land. This was the reason their temple had been burned to the ground. It was because of their sin that their governor Gedaliah was murdered. The only appropriate reason to fast was in repentance for their sin and rebellion. They had been fasting because of what they had lost; whereas, God wanted them to fast because of their sin. Their hearts were broken because they had lost their temple; whereas, God wanted their hearts to be broken because they had driven him from among them.

God had often spoken to his people, but they had refused to listen. Then God determined in his heart that he would not listen to them. Instead, he cast them away from his presence. He sent them into exile, to a place where they were strangers. He stripped them of their land and their homes. All these things happened because of their sin and rebellion.

What was God telling his people who came to him about this fast of the fifth month? He was telling them that their fast had been hypocritical to start with. They had been fasting and mourning for their own loss, not for their sin. In reality, God did not even recognize their fast. Is it possible that what we think we do for God is really being done for ourselves? Could we be worshiping God only because of what we are getting out of it ourselves? Could we be praying only to prosper ourselves? Is our relationship with God self-centered? What a shock it would be for us to come to the end of our lives and realize that we have not really been serving God at all; instead, we have been serving ourselves. This chapter gives us cause for reflection.

For Consideration:

- Is it possible that we have served and worshiped God like the people of this chapter? Could we be fooling ourselves into believing that we are worshiping God when in reality we are only serving our own interests?

- Is it possible to be serving ourselves in worship? Explain.

- What is God really looking for today in his people?

For Prayer:

- Ask God to open your eyes to see if you have been serving him only for what you can get yourself.

- Ask him to help you to serve out of true love and devotion to him and not out of selfish motives or ambitions.

- Ask him to forgive you for the times you have fallen short of this standard.

11

Blessing Restored

Read Zechariah 8:1–23

We saw in the last meditation that certain men had come to the prophets to seek the will of the Lord regarding the practice of particular fasts. These fasts were in commemoration of the events that took place at the time of Israel's exile to the land of Babylon.

In the last chapter, God told his people how their fathers had turned away from him so that he had been forced to discipline them for their evil ways. In chapter 8 the tone changed. The Almighty stated: "I am very jealous for Zion; I am burning with jealousy for her" (verse 1). It should be understood that these people did not deserve the Lord's jealousy for them. In the last chapter, we saw how their actions had not been pleasing to him. They had been fasting, but their fasting was only for themselves. They were not repentant for their sin. Despite this the Lord had a deep feeling of jealousy for them. He longed to have them for himself. His desire was that they belong to him. What an incredible thing it is to know that the Lord is jealous for us and our affection. He longs to come to us and bless us. He is not a God who is far off. He wants to be very near to us.

Through his prophet Zechariah, the Lord told his people that he would return to the city of Jerusalem and dwell there. It is important for us to note that God does remove his presence at times from his people. There are various reasons for this. Sin is the greatest obstacle to the presence of God. God had removed his presence from the city of Jerusalem and from his people for a time so that they would understand their need of him. Then God was going to return to them.

When God returned to Jerusalem, the city would be called the "City of Truth" (verse 3). The mountain on which that city was built would be called the Holy Mountain because that was where the Lord's presence was being manifested. What a wonderful thing it is to know the presence of the Lord in this way. Notice the result of the Lord's coming to the city of Jerusalem.

Verse 4 tells us that once again people of a ripe old age would sit in the streets of Jerusalem. Each of them would have a cane because of old age. Old age was considered a sign of blessing in the city of Jerusalem. Had the blessing of God been removed from them, they would not have lived long enough to see their golden years. They would have died in their youth.

As for the youth, the streets would also be filled with young boys and girls playing. This was a blessing in two ways. First, it meant that the Lord had blessed the wombs of the women of the land to be able to produce these children. Second, it meant that the streets were safe enough for these children to play there. If there were dangers in the street, the children would not be out playing. Again, this was evidence of the rich blessing of the Lord.

The very thought of these blessings was too much for the people to understand. Having just come out of exile, they could hardly imagine having prosperity and security in their own land. To imagine that in their land they would grow old and see their children playing in the streets in safety and security was almost too much to believe. This may have seemed too marvelous for the people to imagine, but it was not too difficult for the Lord to accomplish.

God promised to save his people from the countries around them. He would deliver them from the oppression they were experiencing. They would again be his people, and God would be faithful and righteous toward them (verse 8). Many believers view verses 7 and 8 as referring to a future worldwide regathering of the nation of Israel. The return from Babylon may not be in view because Israel was not scattered to the West until the Roman persecution of the first century AD. A physical and spiritual restoration was here promised to the nation of Israel by God's sovereign hand and by his faithfulness to his everlasting covenant with his chosen people.

With the promise of such a glorious future secured by God's faithfulness, the people should have been motivated to obedience for the task at hand—completing the work of rebuilding the temple. God spoke specifically to those who had seen the foundation of this new temple laid. Through Zechariah the Lord challenged these people to take courage and be strong so that the temple of the Lord would be completed by their hands. God reminded them in verse 10 of a recent time when he had disciplined them for ceasing work on the reconstruction. At that time there was no money in the land. In those days they could not even go to work in safety. The enemy surrounded them. They did not get along with their neighbors. The blessing of God had been removed from their presence, and they were left to themselves. The remembrance of those days was very real in the minds of the people to whom Zechariah spoke.

God reminded them here, however, that those days were

passed. God promised to deal with his people as he had done in the distant past when they were a glorious nation. His blessing would again return to the land (verse 11). The seed would grow in the ground. The vine would yield its fruit. The ground would again produce crops. The heavens would be opened to them so that the dew of God's blessing would again cover their land. God would give these things as an inheritance to his people.

They had been an object of cursing to the nations around them, but they would become a blessing. They were not to be afraid. They were to take courage and persevere in the work that God had called them to do. God reminded them that just as he had determined to bring disaster on them because of their sin, he also determined to bring blessing on them (verses 14–15). They were to take courage and be strong because God promised to be with them and bless them.

Notice that this blessing came with a requirement on God's part. If they were to continue to experience this blessing, they were going to have to live in obedience to a fourfold requirement (verses 16–17).

Speak the truth to one another. Honesty and sincerity of character were essential if they wanted to continue to experience the rich blessing of God. They could not receive from God what they were not willing to give to their neighbors. Lying, deception, and hypocrisy were to be banished from among them.

Render true judgment. They were to be honest not only in what they spoke to each other but also in their testimonies in their courts of justice. Truth and justice were to prevail in the land. Evil was to be destroyed. The rich and the poor were to be given the same treatment. Everyone in the land was to be treated fairly.

Do not plot evil against your neighbor. They were to deal with their neighbors with love and respect. They were to seek the good of their neighbors and never be the cause of their harm.

Do not love to swear falsely. They were to be individuals who kept their word. They were to do what they said. They were to live in such a way that people could trust their intentions.

Notice here that God was very concerned about how they treated each other. His blessing would continue as long as they were living in harmony with each other. God would not pour out his blessing on those who refused to bless his children. Broken relationships in the body of Christ can hinder the flow of God's blessing to the body. We need to be very careful in our dealings with our brothers and sisters in Christ. To dishonor them is to dishonor God and ultimately to remove ourselves from the blessing of God.

In verse 19 the Lord finally answered the question that the people had asked him in chapter 7. They had asked if they were to continue to fast in the various months, as they had during their exile. The fourth month was when the walls of the city had been broken down. The fifth month was when the temple had been burned. The seventh month was when their governor Gedaliah had been murdered. The people had been commemorating these days by fasting and mourning. The Lord declared that their fasts should become joyous celebrations. They no longer needed to remember the bitterness of exile. They needed to celebrate God's goodness, truth, and peace.

The Lord told his people that the days were coming when people would invite each other to seek the Lord God. People of powerful nations would come to Jerusalem to seek the Lord and to entreat him. People from all languages and nations would take hold of a Jew by the hem of his garment and say: "Let us go with you, because we have heard that God is with you" (verse 23). Notice how the nations would beg the Jews to have the privilege of coming with them to meet their God. The Jews wouldn't have to beg the nations to come. The nations would come to them.

Some believers see verses 20–23 promising a time when Jerusalem would be no longer just the heart of Judaism but the peaceful, Christianized worship center of God's dealings with all the world's nations. The nations would come to Jerusalem seeking Jews, not to persecute them but to share in the religious privileges of the Jews with whom God dwelled. This would be an earthly and glorious realization of the ancient promise given to Abraham (Genesis 12:3).

What a wonderful blessing was promised here to God's people. They had suffered tremendously under the discipline of God in the past, but they were going to experience his rich blessing in a glorious future. God was going to do a work that they would find almost impossible to believe. What an encouragement this would have been to his people at this discouraging point in their history.

Could God do the same thing in our day? Could God do a work in our midst that we would have a difficult time believing? Has God changed in his desire for his people? Has his program changed for the expansion of his kingdom? Is it not possible that he wants to do the same today?

For Consideration:

- Do you think that God experiences jealousy for his people today?

- What keeps the blessing of God from your church or your personal life today?

- What evidence of God's blessing can be seen in your life, church, or society today?

- How has God turned your mourning into joy and celebration?

- Why don't we expect God to do great things among us?

For Prayer:

- Thank God for the work that he wants to do in your life today.

- Ask him to reveal to you the obstacles that stand between you and this blessing.

- Ask him to reveal his presence in your life and in your church so that people would know that God is with you and come to him.

- Thank the Lord that, though we do not deserve it, he loves us with a jealous love.

12

Jewels for a Crown

Read Zechariah 9:1–17

I n Zechariah 9 the prophet spoke to the regions of Hadrach, Damascus, and Hamath. These cities were located in the nation of Syria. The Lord was against the land of Hadrach, and God's word would come to rest on the city of Damascus. When God's word came to rest on a place, it brought with it conviction and judgment. That word of judgment would spread throughout the region of Syria and conquer it.

Verse 1 tells us that all eyes were on the Lord. God was going to do something. His people waited in silence for his hand to move. Syria would know his judgment.

Zechariah spoke next to the region of Tyre, which was a great commercial center. This city had built great strongholds. She had within her walls many who were very skilled. Through the use of these skills, they had made the city very powerful and influential. They heaped silver and gold like the dirt on the street. Tyre was a very wealthy and prosperous city, but the Lord would take away her possessions. He would destroy her power on the sea and consume her by fire (verse 4).

As powerful as Tyre was, she would be destroyed, and her wealth would perish with her. She had everything she could ever want in this world, but she was not right with God. Because she was not right with God, she would perish.

The Philistines were addressed in verses 5–7. The great Philistine city of Ashkelon would have cause for fear. She would be deserted. Gaza would writhe in agony. She would lose her king. Ekron's hope would wither away. Foreigners would one day occupy Ashdod. The pride of the Philistines would be cut off because God would come to judge.

Verse 7 tells us that God would take the blood from their mouths. The children of God were forbidden to eat blood. These Philistines were unclean before God, but God would remove this uncleanness from them. The forbidden and unclean food would be removed from between their teeth. God would judge and cleanse this nation, and those who remained would belong to God and become leaders in Judah.

The Philistines were compared here to the Jebusites (see verse 7). The Jebusites were the pagan inhabitants in the region of Jerusalem. David conquered them and built the city of Jerusalem in that region. Commentators tell us that David did not cast these inhabitants out of the region. This was the case with Araunah in 2 Samuel 24:16. The Philistines would be conquered by God but not completely destroyed. They would one day bow the knee to him and surrender to his purposes. They would one day be counted among God's people.

God was going to do a work among these nations. He would cleanse them and move among them. From these nations that were enemies to the people of God, he would draw out a remnant for himself. He could have destroyed them completely, but in love he reached down instead and brought them to himself. How thankful we need to be today that God is a God of unmerited favor. As for his own people, the Israelites, God had not forsaken them. He promised in verse 8 to defend them from the forces that came their way. The oppressor would not be allowed to overrun his people because God would keep watch over them. History shows that, although God did protect Israel from the conquering forces of Alexander the Great, the armies of Rome did come to occupy and persecute the Jews. Therefore, verse 8 must look to a future fulfillment.

In verse 9 God called the daughters of Zion to rejoice. The daughters of Jerusalem were to shout aloud. The day was approaching when their king would come and reign in righteousness. He would come not only with salvation from their enemies but also salvation from the consequences of sin and separation from God. Their king would be gentle and humble. He was described here as coming on a donkey, a humble and peaceful animal.

Commentators tell us that it was not unusual for an ancient king or a prince to ride on a donkey. The donkey was significant because it was an animal of peace. When the Bible speaks of the Lord coming on a horse, it is to exercise judgment (Revelation 19:11). The donkey here is in contrast to the war horse. This king who would come to them would be a king of peace. Verse 10 tells us that he would take away the chariot from Ephraim and the war horses from Jerusalem. He would break the battle bow and proclaim peace to the nations. His rule would be from sea to sea and from the river to the ends of the earth. The river in verse 10 probably referred to the Euphrates River. It was in this area that the Garden of Eden was located. From that starting point to the ends of the earth, this reign of peace would be extended.

This chapter clearly prophesied the coming of the Lord

Jesus. He came to extend his reign of peace with God to the far corners of the earth. Every day Christ's spiritual kingdom is expanding. People from every nation and tribe are bowing the knee to him as their Lord and Savior. We are seeing a spiritual fulfillment of this wonderful prophecy in our day. As believers we are part of the fulfillment of this prophecy.

Attention shifted in verse 11 to the Israelites. God intended to do a wonderful thing through them as his covenant people. The Lord would extend his reign of righteousness from Israel to the ends of the earth. Because of the blood of the covenant, he would not forget them. He would take them out of the watery pit and restore them to himself. God would not forget what he had promised to Abraham.

He called his people who were still in exile to return to the fortress (verse 12). The fortress was a reference to the city of Jerusalem, where the Lord was going to reveal his presence in power. A call went out for his exiled people to return to their homeland to experience the rich blessings of God. God promised them a double portion of blessings from his hand. God was not blind to their suffering. He would bring a double blessing to them.

The presence of God would be very evident in their midst. God tells us that he would bend Judah like a bow and fill it with Ephraim. Judah would be a bow in the hands of the Lord, and Ephraim would be his arrow aimed at Israel's enemies to destroy them. In this particular case, Greece was seen as the enemy (verse 13). As a divine warrior, God would use his people like a sword in his hand to conquer the Gentile nations and bring peace to the earth.

God's people would be powerful in his hands. God would appear over them, and his blessing would be on them. His arrows would flash like lightning. His trumpet would sound and he would march in the storm. There is a sense here of the awesome presence of God as he moved with his people. They would become a powerful and awesome people because he was among them.

The Lord God would shield his chosen people. With him at their side, they would overcome their enemies with slingshots (verse 15). This was the weapon that David used to overcome Goliath. While the whole army had feared this giant, David went in the name of the Lord and conquered Goliath with a single stone from a brook. Small things become big in the hands of God. Israel would drink and roar as with wine and be full like the bowl of blood used for sprinkling the altar. The picture here was of Israel advancing with all boldness into victorious battle. God's people would be mighty and powerful because God was with them.

The Lord God would save his people. They were his flock, and he was their shepherd (verse 16). He would gather them together like jewels for a crown. They would sparkle and shine for him. He would proudly display them as his trophies. As a king proudly displays the jewels on his crown, so the Lord would proudly display his children to the world. What a picture. How he delights in his people, who are precious and valuable like jewels in a crown. You are one of those jewels and I am one, too. And "on that day" Judah and Ephraim will again be saved. They will be the Lord's flock and "sparkle in his land."

Listen to what God said about those jewels in verse 17, "How attractive and beautiful they will be!" How did those jewels get to be so attractive? They had to go through the fire of affliction and suffering. They were tested in the furnace of trial. Their suffering made them stronger and more beautiful, and the grain and new wine of his blessing would make them thrive.

We understand from this chapter that God had a wonderful plan for his people. They would be tried and tested, but it was only to make them more beautiful. They were to become like the jewels for a crown. In him, they would be powerful. In him they would be shielded and protected. God had a wonderful plan and purpose for Israel, as he does for all of us. Our trials will only make us better and more beautiful.

For Consideration:

- God's people are called to rejoice and shout for joy in verse 9. What reasons do we have as believers to shout for joy?

- Notice in verse 10 that the Lord promised to speak peace to the nations, even to the enemies of his people. What comfort do you take from this for your own nation and city?

- God's people were strong in him, but his presence was not always manifested with power. What kept God from manifesting his power in his people?

- What comfort do you take from the fact that God's people are like the jewels of a crown?

For Prayer:

- Thank the Lord for the promise that in him we are strong. Ask him to help you remain in him.

- Are there people you know who need to see a powerful work of God in their lives? Ask God to reveal himself to them.

- Thank God that he considers us beautiful, like the jewels of a crown. Thank him for the trials that made you into the jewel you are today.

13

Spring Rain

Read Zechariah 10:1–12

Having reminded his people in the last chapter that they were beautiful and precious, like jewels in a crown, the Lord challenged them to ask him for the spring rains. The spring rains were necessary to assure that there would be a good harvest. The spring rains should be understood to symbolize the blessing the Lord wanted to pour out on his people. God wanted his people to ask him for these blessings.

How often we have believed deep in our hearts that we have to struggle to convince God to pour out his blessing on us. Sometimes we feel that we have to do certain things or meet certain standards before we can expect anything from God. This verse is a real challenge to this way of thinking. God is calling us to ask him for the spring rain. He is more willing to pour out his blessing on us than we are willing to receive that blessing.

Notice also in verse 1 that the Lord makes the storm

clouds and gives showers of rain to people and the plants of the field to everyone. God is the source of all blessing. He is willing to dispense his gifts to whomever will ask him for them. Notice here that he gives the plants of the field to everyone. You may not feel worthy, but God is willing to give. The challenge here is for us to ask. We will not receive if we do not ask (James 4:2).

God's people were unfaithful to him. They had idols, but these idols could not speak to them. They had diviners who saw visions and dreams, but these were lying visions and false dreams that gave vain comfort to the people of God. God's people were left wandering like sheep without a shepherd (verse 2).

God knew what was happening to his people, and it grieved his heart. In verse 3 he told his people that his anger was going to burn against these false shepherds. He would punish the leaders of his people who were not taking seriously their role as shepherds. How seriously we need to take this role as leaders of God's flock. Not to care for his flock is to invite the wrath of God on us. God cares deeply for the sheep he has entrusted into our care. He will hold us accountable for their lives.

Notice in verse 3 that because the shepherds were not caring for the sheep, God himself would care for them. The remainder of this chapter Zechariah prophesied about the blessings that the Lord promised to pour out on his people as their Great Shepherd. Let's examine these blessings one by one.

I will make them like proud war horses (verse 3). God promised that as their shepherd he would make his people like proud war horses. These horses were not afraid of battle. They were filled with courage and charged into battle with strength and boldness. This was what the Lord was going to do for his people. He was going to fill them with courage to face the struggle before them. He would make them strong for the approaching battle.

Is this not our role as shepherds? Is it not our responsibility to fill God's people with courage and equip them to face the battle before them? The sheep need the courage of the Lord to stand against the enemy each day. As shepherds, it is our responsibility to build that courage in them.

From Judah will come the cornerstone (verses 4–5). God promised in verse 4 that from Judah would come the cornerstone, the tent peg, the battle bow, and every ruler. What does each of these objects represent?

The cornerstone was considered to be one of the most important stones in a building. Jesus himself was compared to a cornerstone (1 Peter 2:6). This could be a reference to the fact that out of Judah would come the Messiah, the Savior for the world. A cornerstone represented stability. Could it be that the Lord would not only give his people courage but also establish his people to become cornerstones in the great worldwide work he was doing? They would be the foundation on which he would build his work.

The tent peg was what stabilized a tent and kept it from blowing away in a storm. The tent peg was a symbol of perseverance and endurance. When a storm raged, these pegs remained strong and dependable. As the Good Shepherd, God was going to produce sheep that were dependable. His desire was to make them strong and persevering. He was not interested in a people who were going to fall prey to every wind. He wanted a people who would be anchored firmly, a people who would remain true no matter what happened, a people who could withstand the storms of life.

The battle bow was a symbol of war. God was interested in producing a people who were warriors. He was interested in a people who would stand up against the enemy and fight. He wanted a strong and courageous people who would not run away the moment the enemy appeared.

Notice also that the Lord wanted to produce rulers from these sheep. He wanted to produce individuals who could themselves lead his people. Once again, is this not the responsibility of the shepherd? Is it not our responsibility to so nurture the sheep that God has entrusted to our care that out of them come stable cornerstones in the body of Christ? Individuals who, like tent pegs, stand firm when the winds of opposition rage around them, people who, like the battle bow, are equipped to face the enemy, people who themselves are leaders. What an awesome responsibility the shepherd has.

God reminded his people in verse 5 that, under his leadership as the Good Shepherd, they would be like mighty warriors. He would produce a people who would go out to the battle and trample the muddy streets. Because the Lord was with them, they would fight and overcome the enemy horsemen. They would be a conquering and victorious people.

I will strengthen the house of Judah (verse 6). The Lord would strengthen the house of Judah and save the house of Joseph. God would do this because he had compassion on his people. For some time they had been in exile. They had been under the heavy hand of God's discipline, but they had been forgiven. It would be as though they had never been rejected at all. God would be their God and draw close to them. Communion with the Lord would be restored, and he would again hear and answer their cries.

Ephraim will become mighty (verse 7). In those days the Lord would so bless the Ephraimites that they would become mighty men. Their hearts would be lifted up in joy and thankfulness to God. There would be joy and rejoicing in the land again as God moved in power and blessing.

I will gather them in (verses 8–10). The time of exile was over. The Good Shepherd would redeem them from the hand of their enemies. He would restore them to the full blessing they once knew in him. His call went out to return to him and be restored to fellowship. The Lord would bring his people out of the lands of their bondage. From Egypt and Assyria, all who had been exiled were being summoned to return. Verse 10 tells us that those who returned would be so plentiful that there would be no room for them. The blessing of the Lord would be so great that the land itself would not be able to contain it.

The surging sea shall be subdued (verse 11). The day was coming when the surging seas would subside. This sea was a symbol of the struggle and oppression that God's people had been under from such enemy nations as Egypt and Assyria. This sea of opposition would dry up. God would judge Israel's enemies who had been responsible for this oppression.

I will strengthen them in the LORD (verse 12). Finally, God promised that his sheep would be strengthened through the Lord. They would again be strong in him and walk in his ways.

The spring rains were about to fall. God wanted to do a wonderful thing among his people. In the first verse, God challenged them simply to ask him for blessing. Could it be that God wants to do the same today? Could it be that all that stands between God's blessing and us is our willingness to ask him for it and receive it from him?

For Consideration:

- Do you think that the Lord wants to pour out on his people today the kind of blessings outlined in this chapter?

- What do you think stands between us and God's blessings?

- What does this passage teach us about the role of spiritual leaders?

- What does this passage teach us about the desire that God has for his sheep?

For Prayer:

- Take a moment to pray for your spiritual leaders. If you are a spiritual leader, ask the Lord to help you to be a faithful shepherd as outlined in this passage.

- Do you have struggles you are going through right now? Ask the Lord to make you strong like a cornerstone and tent peg.

- Thank the Lord that he does desire to bless you and shape you into a clean vessel for his use.

14

The Rejected Shepherd

Read Zechariah 11:1–17

I n chapter 10 we saw the wonderful promises God had for his people. He promised that he would come to shepherd them. He promised that he would pour out his spring rain on them. They would be strong and powerful again. In chapter 11 the tone changes to judgment.

The prophecy recorded in chapter 11 began with wailing. Lebanon was called on to open her doors so that the fire of God's judgment could come on Israel. The pine trees of the land were commanded to wail because the cedar trees had fallen. If the stately cedar tree had fallen, how long would it be before the lowly pine tree fell? The oaks of Bashan too were to wail because the dense forest had been cut down. The shepherds of the land wailed because the rich pasturelands had been destroyed, and there was no place to pasture the sheep. Even the lions felt this devastation as they roared in what used to be the lush thickets of Judah. These thickets too had been ruined.

The picture painted here was one of absolute devastation in the whole land of Israel. Something had swept through the land and laid it waste. This was cause for deep pain and anguish on the part of the people of God. We might wonder what has caused such devastation in the land that had been promised so much blessing in chapter 10. The remainder of the chapter described the cause of this devastation.

In verse 4 a call went out to pasture the flock marked for slaughter. God had been watching what was happening in Israel. The buyers slaughtered the sheep but were not called to account for their actions. Those selling the sheep praised the Lord because they were made rich from selling the poor sheep. Even the shepherds did not care for the sheep. In verse 6 God declared that he would no longer have pity on Israel. Instead, he would hand it over to the neighboring nations (Gentiles). These neighbors would oppress the people of the land, and the Lord would not rescue them. This prophecy described a time of falling away from the Lord and judgment on the land of Israel. This would happen despite the seventy years of exile in Babylon. God's people had not learned their lesson.

The Lord was calling Zechariah to shepherd Israel at a time when the Lord had turned from them. Zechariah was called to go to those who had been marked for destruction. In obedience to the word of the Lord, the prophet Zechariah pastured the flock. He reached out to those who were oppressed and ministered to them in the name of the Lord. Verses 7–14 can be seen as a prophetic drama by Zechariah, representing what would happen to Israel at the time of Christ.

Notice in verse 7 that Zechariah pastured these sheep with two staffs. The first staff was called Favor; the second staff was called Union. Jesus too ministered with these two staffs. He came to demonstrate to us the favor of God and to show us his grace. He also came to minister with the staff of union. His whole ministry was to build a body of believers who would not only be united with God but with each other under this favor of God.

Verse 8 tells us that in one month Zechariah got rid of three shepherds. We are not told who these shepherds were. It may be that the prophet Zechariah got rid of the shepherds spoken about in chapter 10 who were not taking care of the people of God. Notice in verse 8 that the flock grew weary of Zechariah as their shepherd. They did not accept him and his ministry. Zechariah in many ways represented the ministry of the Lord Jesus toward his people Israel. Jesus came as the Good Shepherd to care for his people. He ministered to them, but his own people refused him as their leader. They turned their backs on what he said. Even his own family rejected him and grew weary of his words.

The result of this in verse 9 is that Zechariah said: "I will not be your shepherd. Let the dying die and let the perishing perish. Let those who are left eat one another's flesh." Because they rejected him as shepherd, Zechariah was forced to leave them. This was what happened in the life of the Good Shepherd, Jesus. The Lord Jesus came to offer life to his people, but they rejected him. Zechariah took his shepherd's staff called Favor and broke it in two. This symbolized the end of the Lord's favor and shepherding care that he had provided Israel. It was the Lord who sustained Israel and protected her from foreign invaders. This prophetic drama of Zechariah possibly foretold the destruction of Israel by Rome in AD 70, following Israel's rejection of her Messiah.

In verse 12 Zechariah asked the people for his wages as their shepherd. This was the act of someone who was settling his account on his final day of work. It is interesting that the people weighed out for him thirty pieces of silver as his wage. This obviously was a small and insulting amount to pay a shepherd. Zechariah was told to take this money and "throw it to the potter." These potters were often in the temple making pottery jars for temple use. The act of throwing thirty pieces of silver to the potter prophesied an event in the life of Christ. Matthew 27 recounts the story of the betrayal of the Lord Jesus by Judas. For thirty pieces of silver, Judas sold the Lord Jesus to the Jewish leaders. Judas later felt remorse for this decision and took the thirty pieces of silver and *threw* them to the priests in the temple. Not knowing what to do with this dirty money, the priests bought the *potter's* field.

In verse 14 Zechariah broke the second staff called Union. He had already broken the staff of God's favor. By breaking this second staff, Zechariah prophesied what would happen within Israel after the rejection of Messiah. There would be a breaking down of the union of "brotherhood between Judah and Israel." The passage did not specify how this disunity would take place.

Zechariah prophesied that the day would come when Israel would be handed over to a foolish shepherd (see verse 16). This shepherd would not protect the flock. He would not seek the young or heal the injured or even feed the healthy; instead, his sheep would be his meat. They would be treated cruelly, having their hoofs torn off to satisfy his appetite. Some readers might see here a reference to Jewish leaders such as the Pharisees who came after the time of Christ. Others might see a reference to the Antichrist prophesied in a variety of passages (Daniel 9:27; 2 Thessalonians 2:3–10).

Whoever this evil shepherd was, he would be punished. Because he did not care for the flock, he would be judged. His sword would be struck from his hand and his arm would be withered. His power would be taken from him, and his right eye would be blinded. God would triumph over this evil shepherd in the end. God's people would be misled by a false shepherd because they turned from their true shepherd.

In God's grace, however, he would not forget them as his people. That day would come when God would break the arm of this deceiving shepherd and restore his people to himself.

It is a terrible thing to reject the only hope we have. Right here in this Old Testament passage, we read about how the Jewish people, who had been promised so much, would reject the Lord Jesus. What blessing could have been theirs, but they turned their back on it. While for a time, the rods of favor and union have been broken, there will yet be a reunion. God will not forget his people. Maybe like the Jews of Zechariah's day, you too have wandered dangerously far from the Lord. Today he is willing to restore you to that place of blessing if you will come to him. Don't reject such a wonderful offer.

For Consideration:

- What do we learn here about the wrath of God? Will God punish sin? Is there hope for those who have fallen under his divine judgment?

- Is there an end to the pleading of God? Is there a time when the Lord will stop pleading and make his judgment final?

- What comfort do you take from the fact that the rejection of the Lord Jesus was prophesied in such detail?

- What do we learn here about the grace and compassion of the Lord God?

For Prayer:

- Thank God that he opened your eyes to the reality of the Lord Jesus and his work.

- Thank him that he knows all things and that even the rejection of Jesus was prophesied before it happened. Thank the Lord that nothing takes him by surprise.

- Thank him for his wonderful grace to those who have for a long time turned from him.

15

On That Day

Read Zechariah 12:1–13

Chapter 11 ended on a fairly negative tone. The children of Israel would reject the coming Messiah. Because they would turn their backs on him, God would turn from them for a time. Chapter 12 continued this same theme. We see here, however, that God would not abandon the Israelites forever.

A word from the Lord came to Zechariah concerning Israel in verse 1. God introduced himself as the Lord who stretched out the heavens and founded the earth. He formed the spirit of mankind and is the creator and sustainer of life. Nothing can stand against him and his purposes. What he has determined will ultimately happen.

This awesome God spoke through his servant Zechariah: "I am going to make Jerusalem a cup that sends all the surrounding peoples reeling" (verse 2). How was this going to happen? It would begin with the nations besieging Judah and Jerusalem.

This reference to the besieging of the city of Jerusalem could not have referred to the Babylonian siege and captivity. One view is that this was a prophetic word about what would happen to those who came back from exile in Babylon. They would remain for a time in their land, but they would be taken captive later by the surrounding nations. Historically, we know that the Greeks and the Romans would come and invade the land of Israel and oppress the people of God. By the time the Lord Jesus came to this earth, the land of Israel was under Roman domination. Another view is that these verses referred to a period of divine favor for Israel and divine judgment of the Gentile nations, which would precede the establishment of Christ's earthly kingdom.

The phrase "on that day" was repeated at least six times in this one chapter. This chapter was devoted to the description of those days in the future when the land of Israel would be under the domination of these foreign lands. Verse 3 tells us that on that day when the nations of the earth would gather against Israel, God would make Jerusalem an immovable rock for all the nations. All who tried to move it would be injured. While God did not promise freedom from trial and difficulty for his people, he did promise to keep them. For a time they would be disciplined, but God would not completely abandon them. He still had a purpose for them.

In those days of oppression by the enemy nations, God would strike the horses with panic and the enemy riders with madness (see verse 4). God would blind the horses of the nations so that they could not overcome his people. In the days of Abraham, the men of Sodom and Gomorrah tried to force their way into the home of Lot (see Genesis 19). The angel of the Lord struck these men with blindness so that they could not overcome Lot and his family. This was what Zechariah said would happen to the enemies of God's people.

What an encouragement it is for us to see what the Lord would do for his people. It was true that they would reject the Messiah. They would turn their backs on him. They would, for a period of time, be judged by God. Despite this, however, they would still be cared for and protected by God in some ways. He would discipline them, but he would not abandon them. Do you have a loved one who is in this situation? Have they wandered away from the Lord? There is encouragement here for us. God will care for them. He will not abandon them in their rebellion. He will watch over them and keep them.

The day was coming when the Lord would return to Israel. He would again strengthen them, and they would know that he was among them (see verse 5). On that day the Lord would make the leaders of Judah like a firepot in a woodpile. They would burn brightly, consuming the nations around them. Like a flaming torch among the sheaves of grain, they would consume their enemies. Those who would come to oppress them would be destroyed in the fire of God's vengeance. Jerusalem would remain intact. Though she would suffer much and be severely attacked, God would not allow her to be removed. He would be faithful to his promise. We see even in our day the fighting that has gone on over the years over the city of Jerusalem. This prophecy of Zechariah has remained true.

Verse 7 tells us that on the day when the Lord delivered his people, he would deliver the dwellings of Judah first so that the people of the house of David and the inhabitants of Jerusalem would not conclude that they were more important to God than the people of Judah. God would treat his people fairly. Like a father who loves all his children, God would not play favorites with Jerusalem. God would defend all of the people in the countryside of Judah as he would defend those who lived in the great city of Jerusalem. The unfortified cities of Judah would be as victorious as the fortified city of

Jerusalem with all her forces. In this deliverance, no human force would receive the glory. The weak and defenseless would be delivered as well as the powerful and strong. God would be no respecter of persons.

In verse 8 the Lord promised to shield those who lived in Jerusalem and strengthen them so that even the feeblest among them would be like David who was Israel's greatest warrior. On that day, God would make all his people like David the mighty warrior. Their enemies would not be able to stand against them. The house of David would be like God, with the Angel of the Lord going before them. The Davidic rulers would be said to be like God in the sense that he was in their midst. The Angel of God was going before them to bless and to strengthen them. To fight against Israel would be like fighting against God himself. No one would be able to stand against God's chosen nation. Verse 9 tells us that on that day God would destroy all the nations that attacked Jerusalem. Israel would indeed reject her Messiah, but God would not reject Israel. He had a sure purpose and plan for Jerusalem. His people would remain special in his eyes.

The day was coming when God would pour out a gracious spirit on his people (see verse 10). He would do a powerful spiritual work among them. God promised through Zechariah to pour out on the house of David and Jerusalem a spirit of grace and supplication. God would shower them with his grace so that they would receive the benefits of his forgiveness and mercy. He would also put within them a spirit of supplication. Their hearts would be moved to cry out to God again. How we need to see that same spirit being poured out on our society today. The hardness of hearts is very real, but God is able to pour out a spirit of grace and supplication. Notice the result of this outpouring.

Verse 10 tells us that God's chosen people would look on him whom they had pierced and mourn for him like one would mourn for an only child who had died. Who is the one they had pierced? This was the Lord Jesus himself. God's spirit of grace would so move among his people that they would be broken because of what they had done in putting the Lord Jesus on the cross. When God poured out this spirit, there would be a recognition of the Lord Jesus and his work. There would be a sense of repentance and grief for sin. This was what God was going to do for his people.

Verse 11 tells us that on the day that God poured out this spirit of grace, the weeping in Jerusalem would be very great. They would weep like the weeping of Hadad Rimmon. There is some debate among scholars regarding the identity of Hadad Rimmon. Some see it as a location in the region of Megiddo. If this is the case, there is evidence that in this area many false gods were worshiped. Could this be a reference to the sound of mourning that could be heard in this area as the worshipers called out to their false gods? A second interpretation would see Hadad Rimmon as the fertility god Tammuz of the Babylonians. Others see this as a reference to the national mourning for righteous King Josiah who died in Megiddo (2 Chronicles 35:20–24). Whichever interpretation is correct, the idea here was that there would be much mourning in the region of Jerusalem. God's people would weep because of the spirit of repentance that he would put within them. God would move them to tears for their sin of rejecting Messiah, the one they had pierced.

Notice in verses 12 and 13 that the Lord would move in revival throughout the entire nation of his people. Each clan would mourn by itself. There was something powerful happening here. People throughout Israel were being brought to repentance individually. There were no big meetings. There was no chance of people getting caught up in the emotions of the moment. Each clan was being touched independently of the others. The Lord was moving and touching each person individually. We can only imagine the power of this wonderful work of the Lord. This prophecy presented great hope for Israel.

We should understand in this chapter that the Lord spoke of a wonderful purpose for the Jews. God would not forget Israel. Zechariah prophesied that there would be a day of revival and repentance for the Jewish nation. God would move in sovereign grace and power and bring them to their Messiah, whom they rejected and pierced.

Be encouraged by this passage. Could it be that the day is coming when God will pour out his presence on your community as well? Will the day come when your community will know this spirit of grace and supplication? Could it be that you too will see the Lord move on you, bringing you the victories you have long sought? There is cause for rejoicing in this chapter.

For Consideration:

- What promise do we have here for those who wander from the Lord?

- What comfort do you find in this passage as you face the struggles and difficulties that are before you?

- Have you experienced this spirit of grace and supplication? What would characterize the person who has received this spirit from the Lord?

- What do we learn here about the purpose God has for the Jews?

For Prayer:

- Thank God that even though we have often turned our backs on the Lord, he has remained faithful.

- Ask the Lord to pour out his spirit of grace and supplication on us again so that we may see the Lord Jesus afresh.

- Thank the Lord that he does not abandon his children.

16

The Death of the Good Shepherd

Read Zechariah 13:1–9

In the last chapter, we saw how the Lord promised to do a mighty work in the life of his people Israel. He would pour out a gracious spirit on them, and they would mourn for the one they had pierced. The prophecy continued with this theme in chapter 13.

The day was coming when a fountain would be opened to the house of David and the inhabitants of Jerusalem. Verse 1 tells us that the purpose of that fountain was to cleanse them from their sin and impurity. Even after a national rejection of their Messiah, the Jewish people were promised that God would do a powerful work of salvation among them. The day would come when the fountain of God's blessing, renewal, and forgiveness would flow among the royal descendants of David as well as among the common people.

In those days the Lord would banish the names of the idols from their land. The work of God would be such that his people would turn from their idols and seek his face alone. They would no longer remember their foreign gods and idols they had served. False prophets and a spirit of impurity would also be removed from the land.

Notice the extent of this cleansing in the land in verse 3. If a false prophet stood up to speak, even his own father and mother would say, "You must die." Because he prophesied lies in the name of the Lord, even his own parents would stab and kill him. This was in accordance with the law of God as recorded in Deuteronomy 13:6–9, "If your very own brother, or your son or daughter, or the wife you love, or your closest friend secretly entices you, saying, 'Let us go and worship other gods' (gods that neither you nor your fathers have known, gods of the peoples around you, whether near or far, from one end of the land to the other), do not yield to him or listen to him. Show him no pity. Do not spare him or shield him. You must certainly put him to death. Your hand must be the first in putting him to death, and then the hands of all the people."

It is hard to imagine a time when the people of God would be so in tune with righteousness that nothing could stand between them and their God. They would willingly turn their backs on their own wicked children in order to honor God. Nothing was to come between them and their God. During most of Israel's history, God's laws were not obeyed. Even in our day, we allow certain sins to remain in our land and our lives. Pastors are sometimes afraid that if they speak out against certain sins, they will lose members of their congregations. We fear that people may turn from us if we rebuke their sin. Often we simply turn our heads and look the other way.

In these prophesied days, however, there would be such a deep sense of the presence of the Lord that the believers would not allow anything to stand between them and their God (not even their own children). Such would be the awesome sense of the presence of the Lord in their midst.

On that day the false prophets would be ashamed of their false prophetic visions (verse 4). They would not put on their prophetic garments of hair. They would not want anyone to know that they were prophets. They would tell people that they were farmers and that they had been farmers from the time of their youth. If asked about the wounds on their body, they would say that they had received these wounds at the home of a friend. In reality, however, these wounds were very likely self-inflicted. The false prophets of the day, like the prophets of Baal in the days of Elijah, would often cut themselves in order to get closer to their demonic gods. We have a clear example of this in 1 Kings 18:27–28, "At noon Elijah began to taunt them. 'Shout louder!' he said. 'Surely he is a god! Perhaps he is deep in thought, or busy, or traveling. Maybe he is sleeping and must be awakened.' So they shouted louder and slashed themselves with swords and spears, as was their custom, until their blood flowed." Here in our passage when the false prophet was asked to account for his self-afflicted wounds, he would lie to protect his life—such would be the fear of the Lord in the land.

Can you imagine a time in your land when the unbelievers would be so ashamed of their sin that they would do anything to keep it from being known? Can you imagine a society where the entertainment industry would be so ashamed of the content of its lewd movies and films that it would take its name off them for fear of being discovered? We can look forward to the time when the Lord will move in such power as he promised here.

How would all this take place? It would not take place in the way the people of Israel would expect. In verses 7–9 we catch a glimpse of the incredible plan of God for the salvation and renewal of Israel.

In verse 7 Zechariah turned from the false prophets to a shepherd. The prophecy began with a call to a sword. "Awake, O sword," cried the Lord God. What was the purpose of this sword? The sword was to strike a shepherd. Notice here in particular what was said about this shepherd. Verse 7 described him as "my shepherd." He was also described as one "who is close to me." This cannot go without notice. The Lord tells us here that the shepherd that was going to be struck was a good shepherd. This was a clear reference to the Lord Jesus who would be crucified for us. Notice also that the shepherd's death was presented as a divine act (see also Acts 2:23).

Notice that when the shepherd was struck, the sheep would be scattered. Jesus took this very passage and applied it to his disciples in Mark 14:27, "'You will all fall away,' Jesus told them, 'for it is written: "I will strike the shepherd, and the sheep will be scattered."'" On the day that they came to arrest the Lord Jesus, his disciples deserted him and fled (see Matthew 26:56). The prophet Zechariah here prophesied that this would happen centuries before the event.

Verse 7 also tells us that the hand of the Lord would be turned against his little ones. All the apostles were persecuted. The early Jewish church knew the impact of this when the enemy was unleashed against them (James 1:1). Persecution broke out against the church as Satan unleashed his evil on them.

Verses 8 and 9 show us the impact of this unleashing of evil on the earth after the crucifixion of the Good Shepherd. Two thirds of the land would be struck down and perish and only one third would remain. This final third would themselves be put through the fire and refined like silver and gold.

The history of the Jewish people has indeed shown us that they have certainly had to go through trial and refining. Nations have risen up against them, and many Jews have perished. God has not abandoned them, however, for there is still a remnant that he holds for himself. After his people were refined, God would answer them. He would call them his people, and they would call him their God. Some believers view verses 8–9 as referring to a future time of great tribulation and refining for the nation Israel. God will save one third of the Jews alive at that time, and they will say, "The LORD is our God" and be restored in their covenant relationship.

In the beginning of this chapter, we saw that God was going to open a fountain that would flow and bring cleansing to Israel. Idols would be cast aside. False prophets would be banished and ashamed of their evil words. How would all this take place? It would take place through the death of the shepherd who would come. This shepherd was the Lord Jesus, and his death, like a fountain, would ultimately cleanse the land of Israel. His death would bring new hope for the people of God. His death would transform their society and bridge the gap between God and his covenant people.

From this side of the cross, we see the transforming power of the crucifixion of the Lord Jesus. Our lives have been changed. We have had victory over our idols and sins. The fountain of his blood has washed us and cleansed us of our evil. Back in the days of Zechariah, some five hundred years before Christ, this prophecy was given to the people of God. This fountain is flowing today, and wherever it goes it brings cleansing and forgiveness. One day it will cleanse the nation of Israel. Have you been cleansed by it?

For Consideration:

- What encouragement do you receive from the fact that the crucifixion of the Lord Jesus was so clearly prophesied so many years before it happened?

- How willing are you to deal with every known sin in your life?

- What difference has the blood of Christ made in your life and the lives of those around you?

For Prayer:

- Thank God for the work he promised to do in the life of his people.

- Ask him to move in power in your life and the life of your church.

- Ask him to help you to be serious about the sin and evil around you.

- Thank him for the death of the Lord Jesus, which sets us free from the power of sin in our lives.

17
Future Blessing

Read Zechariah 14:1–21

In chapter 13 the Lord promised his people that he would send a wonderful revival to the land. Before that day, however, there would be difficult times for the people of God. In verse 1 we read that there was a day coming when their plunder would be divided among them. The New King James Version translates this slightly differently and gives us a general sense of what the verse is telling us: "Behold, the day of the LORD is coming, and your spoil will be divided in your midst" (Zechariah 14:1).

The sense here is that the enemy would come into Israel and take spoils of war. God's people would watch the enemy divide the plunder before their very eyes. In that day the Lord would gather all the nations against the city of Jerusalem. They would fight against it and capture it. The houses of Jerusalem would be ransacked, and the women would be raped. Half the city would go into exile while the other half remained in the ruined city (verse 2).

The Lord would not leave them in this situation, however. Zechariah tells us in verse 3 that the Lord would go out and fight these nations. We are left wondering why the Lord would allow the nations to come against his people in the first place. Why wouldn't he simply protect them from the enemy? Obviously, it was his desire to show them something very important. He wanted to show them and the world that he is an all-powerful and sovereign God.

God will sometimes allow us to suffer in order to show us that he is bigger than that suffering and pain. We very often do not understand the power of God until we have seen the power of the enemy. The Lord lets us see the power of the enemy in order to show us his even greater power. What is encouraging here is that the Lord would rise to fight for his people. He would not forget his own. His timing is not the same as ours. We may have to wait for that deliverance. We may be stretched in our faith and patience, but God will not forget us. He will rise to fight on our behalf.

On the day that the Lord would fight for his people, Zechariah tells us that the Lord's feet would stand on the Mount of Olives, east of Jerusalem (verse 4). The result of this would be that the mountain would split in two, forming a great valley. Half the mountain would move to the north, and half would move to the south. This is very difficult for us to imagine. What is happening here?

The apostle John had a vision of what would happen in the end times, at the end of a period of great tribulation on the entire earth. In Revelation 16 we read an account that resembles what we see here in Zechariah. Listen to what the apostle John saw in his vision as recorded in Revelation 16:16–20: "Then they gathered the kings together to the place that in Hebrew is called Armageddon. The seventh angel poured out his bowl into the air, and out of the temple came a loud voice from the throne, saying, 'It is done!' Then there came flashes of lightning, rumblings, peals of thunder and a severe earthquake. No earthquake like it has ever occurred since man has been on earth, so tremendous was the quake. The great city split into three parts, and the cities of the nations collapsed. God remembered Babylon the Great and gave her the cup filled with the wine of the fury of his wrath. Every island fled away and the mountains could not be found."

There are several significant details in this prophecy of John that we should not miss. John told his readers that the nations would gather together against the Lord (Revelation 16:14). When they came, the Lord would move in power and defend his people. John reminds us that there would be an earthquake like nothing that we have ever seen on the earth. The result of this earthquake was that the city of Jerusalem would be divided into three parts, and the mountains and the islands would disappear. Could it be that what the prophet Zechariah prophesied is the same as what John the apostle saw in his vision?

If Revelation 16 and Zechariah 14 speak of the same events, we should understand that Zechariah was prophesying of a time that is in the future. God's people will still have to go through much suffering. The nations of the earth will one day all rise up against Israel. The Lord will come to earth with great physical signs to rescue his chosen nation.

The reason for the splitting of the Mount of Olives is described for us in verse 5. This newly formed valley would be the means of escape for the people of God. They would escape through this valley in haste, as they did when they fled from the earthquake in the days of Uzziah (Amos 1:1). When his people had escaped, the Lord would come with his holy ones (angels and believers). He would come as a warrior to destroy the enemies of his people. What is clear is that God would first make sure that his people were safe before he would come to exercise his judgment.

There is a very powerful lesson here. God will literally

move mountains to set his people free. Nothing can stand in his way of defending his people. When things seem impossible, God can not only part the water, as he did in the days of Moses, but he can also move the mountains that stand in his way. Whatever your trial is today, you can be sure that the Lord is able to break through and give you victory.

Not only would the Mount of Olives be split, but also we see here that on that day there would be no light, no cold, and no frost. Verse 7 tells us that there would be daylight all the time. Does it strike you as odd that verse 6 says that there would be no light, and verse 7 tells us that it would be daylight all the time? How could it be daylight all the time if there is no light?

Could it be that the light referred to in verse 6 was the light of the sun and the stars, and the light of verse 7 was from another source? Isaiah the prophet spoke of a time when the Lord himself would be the light. We see this in Isaiah 60:19–20, "The sun will no more be your light by day, nor will the brightness of the moon shine on you, for the LORD will be your everlasting light, and your God will be your glory. Your sun will never set again, and your moon will wane no more; the LORD will be your everlasting light, and your days of sorrow will end." The book of Revelation also tells us that in the Holy City of heaven there will be no more sun because the glory of the Lord would light the city (Revelation 22:5).

Verse 9 tells us that in those days the Lord would be king over the whole earth. He would rule over a world that would honor him alone. All other gods would be removed from the land. He would be the light of this world. His glory would light up the streets. Living water would flow from Jerusalem (verse 8). This living water was a symbol of salvation and blessing.

Verse 10 tells us that the region surrounding Jerusalem would be leveled like the plain of Arabah. This seems to correspond with what Zechariah told us in verse 4 about the Mount of Olives splitting. Revelation 16:20 also tells us that the mountains and the islands would disappear. We should understand from this that there will be geographical changes on the earth's surface in the end times.

It should be mentioned here that the city of Jerusalem was noted for the mountains that surrounded the city. These mountains provided a natural defense for the city. In those days, however, there would be no need for this natural protection. God would be the protector, and he would also remove all the enemies of his people. The city of Jerusalem would be inhabited and never again be destroyed. It would be secure. God would protect his own people.

As for the nations, their situation would be very different. The enemies of Jerusalem would suffer the wrath of God. Listen to the judgment against them in verse 12. Zechariah tells us that their flesh would rot while they were still standing on their feet. Their eyes would rot in their sockets, and their tongues would rot in their mouths.

Again, it is interesting to compare what Zechariah prophesied here with what the apostle John saw in Revelation 16:8–11, "The fourth angel poured out his bowl on the sun, and the sun was given power to scorch people with fire. They were seared by the intense heat and they cursed the name of God, who had control over these plagues, but they refused to repent and glorify him. The fifth angel poured out his bowl on the throne of the beast, and his kingdom was plunged into darkness. Men gnawed their tongues in agony and cursed the God of heaven because of their pains and their sores, but they refused to repent of what they had done." Could it be that these two men were speaking about the same event? What is clear is that at the end of time, the enemies of God would be dealt with in all severity. They would be inflicted with great and deadly wounds.

The days of the end times prophesied here would be days

of tremendous panic and fear (see verse 13). In their fright and alarm, people would attack each other. There would be wars and battles, even as the Lord Jesus himself prophesied (Matthew 24:6).

Verses 14–16 prophesy a great battle in which the enemies fight against Jerusalem. Again, this corresponds with the teaching of Revelation 16. John tells us of a great battle in which the enemies of God come together to make war against God and his people. Zechariah prophesied that in that day, Judah would be called to help defend the city of Jerusalem. They would band together to fend off the attack of the enemy. The result of this would be that the wealth of the nations would be collected. Great quantities of gold, silver, and clothing would be amassed. We are told in verse 15 that the plague striking the men and women of the land (verse 12) would also strike the horses, mules, camels, donkeys, and all the animals.

In verse 16 we see that the survivors from the nations that attacked Jerusalem would go up year after year to worship the Lord. They would confess him as Lord and celebrate the Feast of Tabernacles. They would see his power and bow the knee before him as Lord. Notice that these nations would celebrate the Feast of Tabernacles (verse 16).

The Feast of Tabernacles (sometimes called the Feast of Booths) was celebrated each year as a reminder of Israel's time in the wilderness. During this time the children of Israel left their homes and lived in tents or booths made from branches. They did this in remembrance of how they lived in the wilderness. This feast was celebrated immediately after the harvest. It is unclear as to why the nations at the end of time would celebrate this festival. Suffice it to say that the harvest of nations would have occurred. God would have already judged the nations. The people who remained alive after this judgment would be those who bowed the knee to God and wanted to celebrate his goodness. During this Feast of Tabernacles, the people of Zechariah's day had to humble themselves to live in tents made of branches, but they still feasted and celebrated the goodness and bounty of God. The undeserving sinner feasted on the riches of the bounty of God. The picture here is of the nations remembering where they came from but at the same time feasting on the goodness and mercy of God.

Verses 17–19 remind us that if anyone did not go up to worship the Lord in Jerusalem, they would have no rain. If Egypt did not go up to worship the Lord God of Israel, God would send his plagues on her. Some commentators feel that the reason that Egypt is singled out here is because she did not depend on the rain for her agriculture but rather on the Nile River. She could not expect to escape this judgment of God just because she didn't depend on the rain. She too would be punished.

In the days to come, said Zechariah, the words "HOLY TO THE LORD" would be inscribed on the bells of the horses (verse 20). The cooking pots in the Lord's house would be like the sacred bowls in front of the altar. Everything in Jerusalem, even the most common utensils, would be used in service to the Lord Almighty. There would be no Canaanite in the house of the Lord Almighty, only those who gave themselves fully to the Lord God of Israel. Here the term Canaanite represented anyone morally or spiritually unclean.

The cleansing of the land would be so thorough that nothing would be left that was not holy to the Lord. Everything would be dedicated to him and his service. The distinction between the clean and the unclean would not be necessary. Sin would be dealt with once and for all. Nothing sinful or defiled would ever again enter the city. Once again let's compare what Zechariah teaches us here to what the apostle John tells us in Revelation 21:25–27, "On no day will its gates ever be shut, for there will be no night there.

The glory and honor of the nations will be brought into it. Nothing impure will ever enter it, nor will anyone who does what is shameful or deceitful, but only those whose names are written in the Lamb's book of life."

The Lord is going to put an end to evil and sin. The day is coming when he will manifest his triumph over all the earth. While there are still difficult times coming for the people of God, we can be assured of the outcome. God will reign. There is a bright future for Israel and all who worship the King, the Lord of hosts.

For Consideration:

• What encouragement do you get from this chapter regarding God providing a means of escape for you in your time of trouble?

• This section of Scripture speaks of a great cleansing of the earth. What things need to be cleansed in our land today?

• What encouragement do we receive here regarding the victory that is ultimately the Lord's?

• How does this chapter encourage us to move forward in faith?

For Prayer:

• Thank the Lord for the promise here that the day is coming when he will conquer all his enemies.

• Thank the Lord that he does provide a way of escape for us in our times of trouble.

• Ask him to open the eyes of those around you to the reality of what is going to happen in the end times.

- Ask the Lord to strengthen you to face any opposition that might come your way.

Malachi

18

How Have You Loved Us?

Read Malachi 1:1–14

This is the word of the Lord through the prophet Malachi. There is some debate concerning the person of Malachi. The name means "messenger." There is no other reference to this particular individual in the rest of Scripture. This has led some commentators to wonder if this was his real name. Could it be that he chose simply to call himself "the messenger," preferring to remain somewhat anonymous?

It is believed that Malachi lived in the days after the Israelites returned from the Babylonian exile. Because the sacrificial system seems to be well established in this book, it is believed that the temple had been rebuilt and the full sacrificial system renewed. The purpose of this prophecy seems to have been to confront the Israelites with their unfaithfulness and to urge them to pursue holiness and true worship as outlined in the Mosaic Covenant.

Malachi began his message in verse 2. "'I have loved

you,' says the Lord." God's people did not recognize this love, however. "How have you loved us?" they asked. It seems incredible that the people of Israel had returned from their exile, and God had opened the door of blessing for them. Just a few years had past, and already they had become complacent and corrupt, insulting his grace and kindness. How quickly we offend the goodness of God.

Malachi reminded his people of how God had chosen Jacob their father. He loved Jacob and made his descendants into a great nation. God's blessing was on them. On the other hand, he had never chosen to show such love and kindness to Jacob's brother, Esau. Where were Esau's descendants (the Edomites)? As the children of Israel looked around them, it was evident that the Edomites were living in a wasteland. Israel, on the other hand, was being tremendously blessed by God. They had returned from their exile and rebuilt their land. Edom had not experienced the same blessing.

Even the Edomites recognized their own poverty. They were a proud people, however, and claimed that they would rebuild their ruined land. Through Malachi the Lord told the Edomites that this would never happen. They would never become a land like Israel. Edom might rebuild, but God would demolish. They would always live under the wrath of God.

The people of Israel had failed to see the blessing of the Lord God in their lives. How easy it is for us to forget what the Lord has done in us. Are you aware of what the Lord is doing in you? Have you forgotten where he has taken you from? Evidence of the blessing of the Lord is all around. When you are tempted to wonder if God really loves you, open your eyes and look at the wonderful things that the Lord has been doing. When we open our eyes, our hearts will overflow with thanksgiving to God. Instead of wondering if God loved them, God's people should have been praising him for his wonderful care (see verse 5).

What is amazing about this whole chapter is the fact that some fifty or sixty years (according to historians) after the return from exile, the people of God were already returning to their former corrupt condition. Not only were they questioning the love of God for them, there were other problems in the land. Listen to what the Lord said in verse 6: "A son honors his father, and a servant his master. If I am a father, where is the honor due me? If I am a master, where is the respect due me?"

In particular, the priests of the land were guilty of showing contempt for the name of the Lord (verse 6). The amazing thing about this, however, was that the priests did not understand how they were showing contempt for God. "How have we been showing contempt for you?" they asked.

The Lord reminded them of what they had been doing. These priests had been placing defiled food on the altar. They were bringing blind, crippled, and diseased animals to sacrifice to the Lord. The law of Moses was clear on this point: only spotless and unblemished animals could be sacrificed in worship to the Lord. Somehow, these priests came to believe that God would accept second best. They were offering what was left over after they took the best for themselves.

God challenged his people to give these same animals to their governor. Would the governor be pleased with them? If the governor would consider it an insult to be presented with the worst of the flock, why did the people think the Lord would favorably receive them?

What a challenge this is to us today as well. Are we guilty of offering to the Lord our second best? Do we give him what is left over after we have taken all we need for ourselves? The Father gave us his Son, and the Son gave up his life for us. How can we offer to God anything but our best?

The call went out for the people of God to repent and cry out to God for forgiveness (verse 9). Not only was giving God their leftovers an insult, but it was a sin that needed to be confessed. We don't often see things in this way. When we refuse to give God the best we have, we are guilty of sinning against him. We pat ourselves on the back because we have given something to the Lord. We can give to God and still insult him. The quality of the gift reflects what we feel toward God. What does your giving reveal about how you feel toward God? Is he the God you give your leftovers to, or is he the God who deserves the best of your efforts and resources?

God took no pleasure in these defiled offerings. "Oh, that one of you would shut the temple doors," he cried in verse 10. He did not want any more insincere offerings. It was better to stop all pretense of worship than to continue in hypocrisy. Could it be that this is how the Lord sees some of the worship services of our day? When he looks down on us, does his heart rejoice at the wonderful gifts of praise and thanksgiving we are offering him? Does he see individuals who praise him with their lips but whose minds are far away? Do we mock his name? Do we blaspheme him by our pretense of worship? Does he wish that some churches would close their doors in order to prevent more hypocrisy?

The name of the Lord is great and awesome. That name is to be lifted high and honored throughout the earth. These people, however, had profaned it. They did so by saying that the table of the Lord was defiled and that the worship of God was a burden. There was no joy in the service of the Lord anymore. People came to worship out of duty and obligation but not out of love for the Lord. In so doing, they treated the worship of God with contempt. How this grieved the Lord.

Verse 13 tells us that the Lord would not accept their diseased animals. He cursed anyone who vowed to give the best of the flock but chose instead to offer the diseased and crippled. God's name was to be feared. His people were not to dishonor him by offering what was unacceptable in his sight.

We see from this chapter how quickly things deteriorated in Israel after the restoration. Very soon after they returned from exile, the people of God again fell into national sin. The worship of God became a burden. They became more concerned about themselves than they were for the things of God. God's people had consistently failed him. The law had proven itself incapable of leading them to God. They needed a Savior.

For us the challenge of this passage is to examine ourselves before the Lord. Do we offer him the best we have? Are we more concerned about the advancement of his kingdom than our own cause? Has the worship of this great and awesome God become a burden and drudgery to us? How we need to see a mighty move of his Spirit to cleanse us and equip us to serve him as the awesome and mighty God he is.

For Consideration:

• Is there evidence in our land today of a condition similar to the one that Malachi was describing?

• Have you ever been guilty of giving God your second best or your leftovers?

• Take a moment to consider your own worship of God. Do you come to him with joy and delight, or have you found yourselves feeling that worship was a burden to you?

• In what way do our gifts reflect our opinion of God?

For Prayer:

- Ask God to forgive you for the times you have not given your best to him.

- Ask him to enable you to be more willing to give him the best you have.

- Ask God to move in you, bringing renewed zeal for him and the worship of his name.

19

Broken Covenants and Broken Faith

Read Malachi 2:1–16

God had been calling his people to respect and honor him as the awesome and almighty God. That particular challenge went out not only to the people of the land but to the priests in particular.

Malachi addressed the priests here: "If you do not listen, and if you do not set your heart to honor my name, . . . I will send a curse upon you, and I will curse your blessings" (verse 2). These powerful words communicated the intensity of the message that the Lord wanted to get across to his people. If they did not listen to this message, they could expect the curse of God to fall on them.

Notice in particular that the Lord told them that he would curse their blessings. The Lord has certainly richly blessed us as his children. Maybe God has blessed you with physical riches. How long would it take for these riches to become a curse in your life? How many people have been led astray by riches? How many people have seen their faith diminish as they got caught up in the pull of money and possessions? They end up very unhappy people while those around them with almost nothing rejoice in the little they do have.

How do we keep our blessings from becoming a curse? Malachi reminds us here in verse 2 that we can do this by setting our hearts to honor the Lord and place him as the highest priority in our lives. We recognize him as the giver of all blessings and thank and praise him. We also commit ourselves to using the blessings he has given us for his honor and glory. When our hearts are committed to seeking him in this way, our blessings remain fresh. If we do not commit ourselves to honoring him through these blessings, they will quickly become a curse for us. If we want our blessings to remain blessings, we need to keep them in their proper place. We must never let them take God's place in our life. We must always use them for his glory and honor.

In this passage, we have a case where the priests of the land had been blessed by God with a wonderful privilege and position. They were using that position and privilege for themselves and their own glory, not the Lord's. The result was that these blessings were quickly becoming a curse in their lives.

The disregard of the priests for the honor of the Lord had lingering implications in their lives and the lives of their descendants. God told them that he would rebuke their descendants because of their sin. The curse of God would not only affect the priests themselves but their children as well. How important it is for us to understand this principle. When you as a father or mother sin and turn your back on God, your children will suffer for it as well. The impact of your sin can go on for generations until the cycle is broken. This passage seems to make it clear that the sins of the fathers can indeed affect the generations to come. In the Lord Jesus the effect of parental disobedience can be broken. Each generation is given the opportunity to either continue in the rebellious ways of their parents or walk in the blessings of the Lord though obedience and fellowship with God.

Not only would their seed be adversely affected but also these negligent priests would be put to shame. God told them that he would spread the offal of their sacrifices on their faces, and they would be carried off with it. The offal was the internal waste of the sacrificial animal that had to be taken out of the city and burned. This offal was filthy. This was how the Lord saw the priests. They were as unclean as the dung and inner parts of the animals they slaughtered. God would spread the unclean refuse of their sacrifices on the priests' faces and take away their office. The priests were an unclean offense to the Lord.

When these things happened, the priests would know that what the prophet Malachi said was from the Lord. This was the test of the true prophet. If what he said came to pass, it was from the Lord. The problem in this case, however, was that it was too late for these priests. The judgment had already fallen. In verses 5–7 the Lord tells us something about the role of the priest. Let's look at this in some detail.

God made his covenant with him (verse 5). God had entered into a special covenant with the priest. He was set apart to administer God's covenant of peace and life. He was to lead God's people into life and peace with their Creator. What an honor and privilege this was. He was God's special instrument. His life was to be devoted to this cause. That covenant was not to be broken. Nothing was to keep him from being true to his calling. As the Lord's specially chosen instrument, the priest represented God in everything he did. He had been set apart by a special arrangement with God.

The priest was called to reverence (verse 5). As a representative of God, the priest was called to a life of reverence for God's name. He was to stand in awe of the Lord's holy name. He was to take his role seriously. He served an awesome and holy God. His life and words were to reflect his deep respect and reverence for the Lord he served. While every believer is to reverence God in this way, surely his specially chosen servants are to particularly live in that reverence and respect. If you are a Christian leader, people need to see this reverence for God in your every word and action.

True instruction was to be in his mouth (verse 6). The priest was to know the truth of God's Word and proclaim that truth. When he stood up to speak, he was to be careful to speak the truth. He was not to speak his own mind but the word that God gave him. Sometimes that truth would not be accepted. At times the word of God might be hard for people to hear. The priest was not to dilute God's message to make it more acceptable. When some of the prophets spoke God's word, they were killed. The priest too was to be willing to die for the word God was asking him to proclaim. He was not to fear the consequences of delivering God's message.

He was to walk with God (verse 6). Not only was he to speak the truth but he was also to live the truth in his daily walk. The priest was to walk with the Lord in peace and uprightness. This was only possible if he was living in obedience to God and his Word. You cannot walk in peace with God if you are not living in obedience. The priest was to demonstrate to those he served what it meant to live for God.

He was to turn many from sin (verse 6). Verse 6 tells us that as a priest he was to turn many from sin. Like the shepherd who went after the sheep who had gone astray, the priest was to do his utmost to keep those under his authority from falling prey to the attacks and temptations of the enemy. He was to be active when it came to sin. He was not to let his duties slide. When he saw sheep wandering, he was to go after them. This required diligence on the part of the priest. God would hold him accountable to watch out for the sheep and to be sure that they were not being overtaken by sin and the temptations of the evil one.

His lips were to possess knowledge (verse 7). The lips of the priest should have possessed knowledge. Every priest should have known the law of Moses and been able to impart that knowledge to others. When his people did not know what to do, they should have been able come to the priest for guidance and instruction. The priest should have taught the people the wisdom and knowledge necessary to do what the Lord required of them.

He was the messenger of the LORD Almighty (verse 7). The priest was to be the messenger of God to his people. He was to share those things that God put on his heart. He was to be a source of guidance and direction for the people who did not know what to do or where to turn. He was to share the heart of God with his people. He was to bless and encourage them with the word of the Lord and challenge and rebuke them too when it was necessary.

The priests in the day of Malachi, however, had turned from their responsibilities. Their false interpretation of the laws of Moses had caused many people to stumble and fall into sin and rebellion against God. The priests had violated the covenant God had made with their father Levi in setting him and his descendants apart for the spiritual care of his people (see verse 8). Because of this, God caused them to be despised in the eyes of the people. The people had no respect for these priests who had nothing to offer. The negligent priests had succeeded in teaching the people to take the Word of God lightly. These priests showed partiality with the law of God and judged in ways that suited their own needs and desires. People saw this hypocrisy and no longer respected them as spiritual leaders. The people began to wonder why they even needed priests.

The result of this lack of spiritual leadership could be seen in the condition of the nation as a whole. Verse 10 addressed the problem of intermarriage with foreign idol-worshipers. God called his people to recognize that, as a people, they had one Father and one God, who had separated them for himself and made them into a unique nation. Israel was special in his eyes. God's people, however, did not respect this relationship. Instead, they began to marry people who worshiped foreign gods. By so doing they were bringing into Israel those who bowed the knee to idols (Deuteronomy 7:3–6). This led to the corruption of the covenant community and Israelite worship. This practice was blasphemous and showed great disrespect for God's name.

The person who did these things was to be "cut off" from the tents of Jacob (verse 12). Even though people brought offerings to the Lord and did all the right things, they were to be cut off from the people of God if they did not respect God and his ways. These blasphemers were not to be allowed the privilege of calling themselves children of God if they were not willing to stand for him and honor his name in this matter of who they married. The priests appeared to be unconcerned about this issue.

God had something else against his priests. It appears from verse 13 that they were flooding the altar with tears. They were weeping and wailing because the Lord did not seem to be paying attention to their offerings. They grieved greatly over this but failed to understand why God was so distant.

God told them why his blessing was not on them in verse 14. It was because they had been unfaithful to the wife of their youth. God reminded them that as husband and wife they were one flesh and spirit. As such they were to produce a godly offspring. They were to give to their children a heritage of the fear of God so that the next generation would continue in his ways.

These priests, however, had not been faithful to their wives. They were guilty of adultery with other women.

The unfaithfulness of these priests to their wives not only brought the curse of God on their ministries but also drove the presence of God from them. These unholy priests grieved his Holy Spirit. God no longer answered their prayers, and so these priests were powerless.

We cannot underestimate the importance of these verses. The blessing of God was stripped from these priests because they were not taking their role of husband and father seriously. In the New Testament we see that the role of elder was limited to those who had proven themselves in their own family. Our relationship with our spouse and family has a direct impact on our spiritual life. It is important that we be sure to deal with this matter. The priest was expected to be a man who cared for his family and was true and faithful not only to the Word but also to his wife.

It is not the will of God that we neglect our family. It is his sincere desire that we be faithful to the wife of our youth and produce with her a godly offspring that will continue to honor the Lord in the generations to come (verse 15). To fail in this area is to sacrifice the ministry that the Lord has called us to as Christian leaders.

So God called the priest to guard himself in the area of his marriage. That same caution goes out today. You can be sure that the enemy knows how to tempt Christian leaders. How many have already fallen in this area of immorality and unfaithfulness? How devastating it is to the work of God when a pastor or Christian leader commits a sexual sin. Be sure that Satan will tempt you in this area. God called the priest to guard his spirit. Notice the use of the word *spirit* here. Not only were the priests to keep themselves from physically committing the sin of adultery but also they were to guard their minds. This is where it all started. The priests were to recognize the temptations that were before them and to put a hedge around their minds for protection from evil and immoral influences. We too would do well to guard our minds. To guard your mind is to limit what you see and where you go in order to keep yourself from situations where you could be tempted. The word *guard* is an active word. It means that you will have to actually do something about keeping your mind pure, lest you fall into temptation.

God reminded his priests in verse 16 that he hates divorce. This meant that priests were to take their commitment to their wife seriously. They were to work out their problems and deal with whatever might be compromising or destructive to the marriage covenant.

God told his people in verse 16 that he hates a man covering himself with violence. The violence in this context is the violence of divorcing a wife. To divorce is to break one's relationship and covenant. It is to cast a wife aside and leave her ashamed, disgraced, and without provision. This is like covering one's garment with the blood of death. Divorce is a covenantal death and reveals treachery.

Malachi challenged the priests to be honest and pure before the Lord God. The prophet rebuked them because they were not living as God's servants ought to live. They were dishonoring God in their hearts and lives. God called the priests to return to him. He called out to them to realize who they were and who they represented. What an awesome privilege we have to be the Lord's servants. That privilege, however, comes with a great obligation. May God grant that we would be servants who honor him in all we do.

For Consideration:

- Have you ever seen your blessings becoming a curse? Explain.

- How do we keep our blessings from becoming a curse?

- What do we learn from this passage about the role of the priest (pastor)?

- What does God have to say here about the importance of the family and the marital relationship? What impact does this have on our ministry?

- What do we learn here about the importance of guarding the mind?

For Prayer:

- Are you married? Ask the Lord to help you to honor him in your marriage.

- Pray for your pastor as he seeks to exercise the role that the Lord has given him. Ask that God would help him to be faithful in that role.

- Ask God to show you if there is any area of your life that you need to confess and make right.

- Ask the Lord to give you grace to guard your mind and keep you from the temptations that abound around you.

20

Refiner's Fire

Read Malachi 2:17–4:6

G od had been challenging his people with their sins.
In the last chapter, we saw how the Lord spoke
particularly to the priests who, as the representatives
of God, were sadly lacking in their responsibilities and
devotion to him.

It had not taken the people long to turn their backs on
God. Commentators believe that only fifty or sixty years had
passed since the return from exile. Already, God's people
had fallen short of his standard. Here in Malachi 2:17 we
see how the people had been wearying the Lord with their
words. The Israelites did not even have a sense of right or
wrong. The priests had not taught them the truth. They had
not snatched the Israelites away from the flames of their evil
ways. The people were saying that God accepted those who
did evil. They had lost all sense of God's standards. The
result was that injustice abounded in the land.

The question was being asked: "Where is the God of

justice?" (2:17). Things were not very good in the land. People began to question whether God was really in control of things. Was evil going to take over the land?

Are there not times when we begin to ask these questions as well? There are times when it seems that the blessing of the Lord is removed from the land and evil begins to take over. Injustice prevails, and we fail to see God and his justice. This seems to be what was happening in the land of Israel in the days of Malachi.

God had not abandoned Israel. The day was coming when he would indeed move in power. Justice would again prevail in the land. On that day, God would send a messenger to prepare the way before he came (3:1). When that messenger appeared, the Lord, whom they were seeking, would come suddenly to his holy temple.

It is important that we understand what was being said here. The day was coming when God would send a messenger to prepare the way for the coming of the Lord Jesus to his temple. There can be no doubt about the interpretation of this verse. The Lord Jesus himself interpreted this for us in the Gospel of Matthew. Speaking about John the Baptist, Jesus stated in Matthew 11:10: "This is the one about whom it is written: 'I will send my messenger ahead of you, who will prepare your way before you.'"

If John the Baptist was the messenger that God would send, then the Lord Jesus was the one who would come to dwell in their midst. Notice in verse 1 that the Lord was described as the messenger of the covenant whom they desired. The people of God had for many years been seeking the Messiah. It had been prophesied that this Messiah would bring with him a new covenant. The old covenant had only proved that humanity was incapable of serving God as he required. Jesus would come with a new covenant, under which God's people would experience forgiveness and grace. They would be empowered by his Holy Spirit to serve him in a way they had never served him before.

The day of the coming of the Messiah, however, would not be as the people of God expected. "Who can endure the day of his coming," asked Malachi (3:2). Messiah would come like a refiner's fire and a launderer's soap. The coming of the Messiah was for the purpose of dealing with the sins of his people. He would not come to pat them on the back and tell them they were doing a wonderful job. He would come to confront them with their sin and evil ways. He would purify them of their contamination. He would wash them of their uncleanness and refine them in his fire.

Notice in Malachi 3:3 that this purifying would take place among the Levites. As God's representatives, they too were guilty before God. They stood in the service of God, but they were unclean before him. God would refine them like gold and silver. When the Lord Jesus came to this earth, he spoke harsh words to the priests and religious leaders of his day. He often condemned them for their hypocrisy and ungodliness. These were not words the leaders of that day wanted to hear. In the end they would kill Jesus because he exposed their sin and evil.

The Lord promised in verse 3 that he would refine the Levites and re-establish worship. Once again, offerings would be brought to the Lord in righteousness. Judah's offerings would once again be acceptable. This would not be easy, however, because the sin of the land and the leaders would have to be exposed and cleansed. God would refine them and burn out their evil.

Jesus came to refine and purify. Paul, writing to the Ephesians, reminded them of the ministry of the Lord Jesus for the church: "Husbands, love your wives, just as Christ loved the church and gave himself up for her to make her holy, cleansing her by the washing with water through the word, and to present her to himself as a radiant church, without stain or wrinkle or any other blemish, but holy and blameless" (Ephesians 5:25–27).

The desire of the Lord Jesus is to make us holy and present us before the Father without spot or wrinkle. That process of refining is not always an easy thing for us to accept. As he refines us, there are many things that begin to come to the surface. Sins are exposed that we would rather hide and forget. Evil attitudes and thoughts, broken relationships, and sinful habits are challenged. It is the desire of the Lord not only to save us from our sins but also to deliver us from their hold in our lives on a daily basis.

Notice in Malachi 3:5 some of the sins that were being exposed in the land of Israel: sorcery, adultery, perjury, defrauding laborers, oppressing widows and orphans, and depriving foreigners of justice. God saw these sins. The refiner's fire was going to burn away these evils in the land.

Notice in verse 6 that Malachi told the people that it was only because the Lord did not change that the people were not destroyed. He had made a promise to their fathers and he would not go back on his promise. He would be faithful and true to his word and spare their descendants.

The challenge went out for the people to return to the Lord in verse 7. If they returned to him, then he would return to them. If the people refused to listen to the word of the Lord, they would miss the blessings he offered. If they were obedient, his blessing would be on them. Maybe you are wondering why the Lord is not more real to you. Could it be that you need to learn the truth that Malachi teaches us here? Maybe the reason the Lord is not more real to you is because you need to return to him in a certain area of your life. Could it be that you are unwilling to surrender a particular sin? Could it be that you are holding on to something that needs to be surrendered to the Lord before his blessings can be released into your life? "Return to me, says the Lord, and I will return to you" (verse 7).

The people of God in the days of Malachi could not understand what God was saying to them. They asked, "How are we to return?" (3:7). They were blinded to the ways in which they had fallen short of God's standard. Maybe this was because the priest had not clearly taught them the truth. God reminded them of two particular sins that they needed to deal with immediately.

In Malachi 3:8 God spoke to them about their tithe. He accused his people of robbing him. The people could not understand what God was telling them. They saw their money as their own. They went to work and earned their living and felt that they had a right to spend their money as they pleased. God reminded them, however, that the tithe of their money did not belong to them; it belonged to the Lord. God's people could not keep the tithe for themselves. God challenged them to put him to the test in this matter (3:10). He called them to bring their tithes into the temple, as the law of Moses required. God challenged them to examine the results in their lives.

Notice what God promised to those who were obedient to him in this matter of giving: "See if I will not throw open the floodgates of heaven and pour out much blessing" (3:10). He promised a blessing so big that they would not be able to contain it. He promised to prevent the pests from devouring their crops. Their vines would not drop fruit to the ground before their time. The nations around them would call them blessed when they saw the blessing of the Lord on their lives. Their land would be a delightful land to live in (3:12).

We get the distinct impression here that the Lord God wanted desperately to pour out this blessing on his people. One of the things that seemed to hinder this was their disobedience in this matter of the tithe. This same principle applies to our lives as well. It is not that God needs our money, but he wants his people to be involved with him in the advancement of his kingdom on this earth.

This involvement applies to other areas of our lives as well and not just to our finances. God expects us too to give of ourselves for the sake of his kingdom. The Lord addressed the issue of the tithe because it was a particular problem for Israel at this time in their history.

There was another area of sin that needed to be exposed. The Lord accused his people of speaking harsh things against him (see 3:13). Again, his people did not understand what he meant by this. "What have we said against you?" they asked. God reminded them of how they had said that it was futile to serve God. They had also said: "What did we gain by carrying out his requirements and going about like mourners before the LORD Almighty?" (3:14). These questions reflected the general state of faith in the land. The Israelites carried out their spiritual duties with a sense of obligation and not out of love for God. Their spiritual lives were dry and their hearts were far from God.

Notice in verse 15 that they were calling the arrogant and proud blessed. They looked around them and saw how the evildoers seemed to be getting away with sin. They saw individuals who challenged God and were not immediately judged. All these things caused them to wonder where God was. Because of this, they began to ask themselves whether there was indeed any reason to be faithful to God. What profit was there for them in serving God when even the evildoer seemed to prosper?

Again, we see the condition of the spiritual lives of God's people. Could it be that God was putting them to the test? Could it be that he wanted to see who would serve him and who wouldn't? Would they serve God when doing evil brought prosperity? Would they serve God if he did not seem to punish evil immediately? What was their motivation for serving God? Would they serve him when everything was going badly? Would they be faithful even when everything seemed to be falling apart? Could it be that the Lord allowed evil to prosper for a time to see who would serve him out of love?

As Malachi spoke this word to the people of God, there were some who were genuinely touched. They listened to what the Lord was saying through the prophet. They gathered together and spoke to each other about the sins and shortcomings of their nation. God saw their repentant hearts and wrote their names in his "scroll of remembrance" (3:16). The individuals who repented would be remembered in the day the Lord made up his "treasured possession" (3:17). God's grace would be extended to them even as "a man spares his son who serves him." God would look on these individuals with favor and blessing. On the day he came to gather his people to himself, there would be a clear distinction made between those who were righteous and those who were evil and between those who served God and those who did not. Justice would prevail in the end.

The people of God had been wondering what profit there was in serving God. The Lord answered this question in chapter 4. On the day that he would come to gather his children, they would see what profit there was in living for him. It is true that here below there are times when we may not see the difference between those who love the Lord and those who do not. There are times when it seems that evil people are blessed and live with less stress and turmoil than the righteous. In the end, however, God would make a distinction between those who were his and those who were not. God would ultimately separate the sheep from the goats (Matthew 25:31–46).

The prophecy of Malachi ended with a very clear warning. The day was coming when God would burn like a furnace in judgment. The distinction would be made between the righteous and the wicked. All the arrogant and every evildoer would be like stubble. They would be destroyed by the fire of God's judgment and wrath (4:1).

So complete would be this destruction that not a single evil root or branch would remain. God would thoroughly cleanse the land and judge the sinner. While we have not seen the fulfillment of this prophecy, we can be sure that the day is coming when God will cleanse this earth of sin and evil. He has yet a wonderful work of cleansing to do.

As for those who revered his name, things would be very different. The sun of righteousness would rise with healing on his wings (4:2). A new day of blessing and healing was coming for those who loved the Lord. They would be healed from the effects of sin and enter the presence of their Lord. They were pictured here as calves that had been locked up in the stall. When the door opened, they ran out and leaped for joy in their newly found freedom. They would be set free from the bondage of this earth. Joy and blessing would be their portion.

In those days those who belonged to God would be a victorious people. They would trample down the wicked. The wicked, who seemed to prosper, would become like ashes beneath the feet of the righteous (4:3). Until that day believers were called to live in obedience to God and his Word (4:4). They were not to give up serving him even if things did not seem to be going their way. God would reward them in the end.

Malachi gave the people of God a sign of the coming of the Lord. He told them that the Lord would send his servant Elijah before the dreadful day of the Lord (4:5). Jesus identified this Elijah as John the Baptist in Matthew 11:13–14, "For all the Prophets and the Law prophesied until John. And if you are willing to accept it, he is the Elijah who was to come."

The Lord promised that when he came, he would restore the peace and harmony that God intended. He would restore the fathers to the children and the children to the fathers. The impact of his reign would be felt in homes and families of the land of Israel. As the hearts of the fathers would be broken by the power of God, they would in turn give themselves to their families. As God reached out and touched the hearts of the children of the land, they would return to their fathers and live in respect and obedience again. God's grace and love would span the generations. Many believers think that this societal repentance in Israel refers to the time when Messiah returns to Jerusalem to set up his earthly kingdom (Zechariah 12:10–14).

Malachi concluded with a warning. If his people refused this work of the Lord through the Messiah, their land would be struck with a curse. The fact of the matter is that anyone who has not accepted the Lord Jesus as Savior is under that curse. Only by surrendering to Christ and his refining work in our lives can we know freedom from the curse of God.

The day is coming when God will judge the world. God will be true to his character and Word. Malachi made it clear that the Lord Jesus is the only answer to human need. He alone can forgive and cleanse us of the effects of our sin. What a fitting introduction to the New Testament.

For Consideration:

• What things need to be refined in your life?

• What is your motivation for serving the Lord? Would you serve him if there were no blessing in serving him?

• Is there evidence of the curse of God on your land today? Could it be that the reason for this is that we are not living in obedience to the Lord and his Word?

• Are you convinced that your name is written in that book of remembrance? When the Lord comes, are you sure to be part of his "treasured possession?"

- What do we learn here about the Lord Jesus and his work?

For Prayer:

- Ask the Lord to reveal to you any sins that keep his blessing from you.

- Thank him for the victory and joy that we have in the Lord Jesus.

- Thank him for the promise of restored peace and harmony. Do you have a brother or sister you have trouble loving? Ask the Lord to restore that relationship and give you peace.

Light To My Path
Devotional Commentary Series

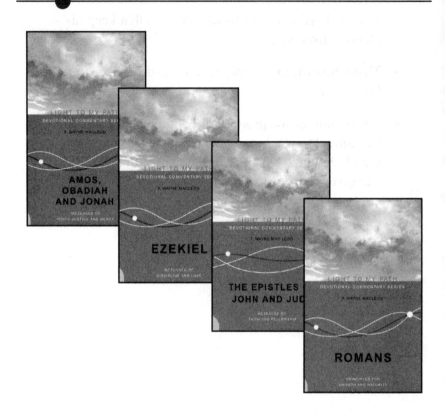

Now Available

Old Testament

- Ezra, Nehemiah, and Esther
- Ezekiel
- Amos, Obadiah, and Jonah
- Micah, Nahum, Habakkuk, and Zephaniah

New Testament

- John
- Acts
- Romans
- The Epistles of John and Jude

A new commentary series for every day devotional use.

―――――――――――――――――――――――――――――――――――●――――――――

"I am impressed by what I have read from this set of commentaries. I have found them to be concise, insightful, inspiring, practical and, above all, true to Scripture. Many will find them to be excellent resources."

Randy Alcorn
director of Eternal Perspective Ministries,
Author of *The Grace & Truth Paradox*
and *Money, Possessions & Eternity*

―――――――――――――――――――――――――――――――――――●――――――――

New in the series
Spring 2005

Old Testament

- Isaiah
- Haggai, Zechariah and Malachi

New Testament

- Philippians and Colossians
- James and 1&2 Peter

Other books available from Authentic Media . . .

Authentic
MEDIA

129 Mobilization Drive
Waynesboro, GA 30830

706-554-1594
1-8MORE-BOOKS
ordersusa@stl.org
www.authenticbooks.com

An Introduction To The New Testament
Three Volume Collection

D. Edmond Hiebert

Though not a commentary, *An Introduction to the New Testament* presents each book's message along with a discussion of such questions as authorship, composition, historical circumstances of their writing, issues of criticism and provides helpful, general information on their content and nature. The bibliographies and annotated book list are extremely helpful for pastors, teachers, and laymen as an excellent invitation to further careful exploration.

This book will be prized by all who have a desire to delve deeply into the New Testament writings.

Volume 1: The Gospels and Acts
Volume 2: The Pauline Epistles
Volume 3: The Non-Pauline Epistles and Revelation

1-884543-74-X   976 Pages

Cat and Dog Theology
Rethinking Our Relationship With Our Master

Bob Sjogren & Dr. Gerald Robison

There is a joke about cats and dogs that conveys their differences perfectly.

> A dog says, "You pet me, you feed me, you shelter me, you love me, you must be God."
> A cat says, "You pet me, you feed me, you shelter me, you love me, I must be God."

These God-given traits of cats ("You exist to serve me") and dogs ("I exist to serve you") are often similar to the theological attitudes we have in our view of God and our relationship to Him. Using the differences between cats and dogs in a light-handed manner, the authors compel us to challenge our thinking in deep and profound ways. As you are drawn toward God and the desire to reflect His glory in your life, you will worship, view missions, and pray in a whole new way. This life-changing book will give you a new perspective and vision for God as you delight in the God who delights in you.

1-884543-17-0   224 Pages

.